THE
Purple BOOK
OF
BOUNDARIES

JASPER EDITION

TIFFANY BUCKNER

© 2021, Tiffany Buckner
The Purple Book of Boundaries
www.tiffanybuckner.com
info@anointedfire.com

Published by:
Anointed Fire™ House
www.anointedfirehouse.com

Cover Design by:
Anointed Fire™ House

Author photograph by:
Photo by: Brand You Brand Nu

Edited by:
Jose Juguna

ISBN: 978-1-7354654-8-7

Note from the Author

Hey you! Thank you for purchasing the Book of Boundaries (Jasper edition). Before you proceed any further into this book series, I want to share my heart with you regarding this series. After having ministered to or counseled countless women about boundary-setting, it became apparent that the issues that are ever-so-prevalent in this world are mainly centered around a need for boundaries. I can truly say that more than ninety percent of the people I've coached, counseled or mentored were in dire straits simply because they didn't have any solid or healthy boundaries set in their lives. In truth, most people have never had anyone to teach them how to properly set boundaries. Consequently, our mental institutions and prisons are overflowing with people whose minds have been taken over by the enemy. All the same, school shootings, racism, divorce, rape, abuse and essentially every evil thing on Earth has been thriving as the human race continues to descend into madness. This is why I created the Book of Boundaries!

You'll notice that there are five parts to this series. They are:
- The Onyx Edition
- The Emerald Edition
- The Sapphire Edition
- **The Jasper Edition** (You are here)
- The Ruby Edition

I chose these names for several reasons, but mainly

because of their colors and what those colors represent. All the same, each of these stones could be found in the ephod of the high priest. "Ye have seen what I did unto the Egyptians, and how I bare you on eagles' wings, and brought you unto myself. Now therefore, if ye will obey my voice indeed, and keep my covenant, then ye shall be a peculiar treasure unto me above all people: for all the earth is mine: And ye shall be unto me a kingdom of priests, and an holy nation. These are the words which thou shalt speak unto the children of Israel" (Exodus 19:4-6). Believers are priests or priestesses of the Most High God, and as such, we should not be in bondage to any person or system that is contrary to our design! This means that these books are all about IDENTITY! They will help you to better understand who you are, and give you the confidence needed to embrace your God-given identity! Once you do this, it will be easier for you to appreciate yourself enough to establish boundaries.

Each of these books represent your exodus from one mindset to another one. You won't just learn about boundaries, but you will learn a lot about yourself while reading this series! You will learn about demonology, relationships and how the enemy advances against the minds of God's people by simply using the technology of ignorance! You will go from black to blue, from not knowing to understanding why it is necessary for you to set boundaries, what it looks and feels like to live behind boundaries, and what you stand to gain once you effectively set and enforce boundaries in your life. You will learn about the infamous narcissist and how to rid your life of that evil force once and for all. This is a must-have book for the sane and the insane! It is designed to help you to take back the real estate of your mind that the enemy has stolen from you!

In this series, I also shared some of my personal stories and dreams with you so that you can also witness the exodus that I had to take from being a mess to a living message! I shared these stories so that you can know that it is POSSIBLE for you to completely leave and annihilate one mindset and lifestyle, and wholeheartedly embrace another lifestyle that looks NOTHING like the one you left behind!

Welcome to the Book of Boundaries! Warning: revelation produces a paradigmatic shift, which causes things in your life that shouldn't be there to wither up and fall away. In other words, if you like being broken, bound and miserable, don't go any further because the revelation in this series is potent enough to sober you up! But if you're ready for a change, flip the page!

Sincerely,
Tiffany Buckner

Introduction

Scriptures for this Edition

And the LORD said unto Moses, Wherefore criest thou unto me? Speak unto the children of Israel, that they go forward: But lift thou up thy rod, and stretch out thine hand over the sea, and divide it: and the children of Israel shall go on dry ground through the midst of the sea.
Exodus 14:15-16

And Moses stretched out his hand over the sea; and the LORD caused the sea to go back by a strong east wind all that night, and made the sea dry land, and the waters were divided. And the children of Israel went into the midst of the sea upon the dry ground: and the waters were a wall unto them on their right hand, and on their left.
Exodus 14:21-22

And the blood shall be to you for a token upon the houses where ye are: and when I see the blood, I will pass over you, and the plague shall not be upon you to destroy you, when I smite the land of Egypt.
Exodus 12:13

But if we walk in the light, as he is in the light, we have fellowship one with another, and the blood of Jesus Christ his Son cleanseth us from all sin.
1 John 1:7

The jasper stone is PURPLE.

The color purple, in this edition, represents royalty; it also represents the mixing of red (the blood of Jesus) with blue (the Word of God). It symbolizes the royal priesthood as established by our King and Savior, Jesus Christ.

In this edition, you will learn more about seasons and how they are affected by your boundaries or lack thereof. In this guide, you will find some of the most profound, revelatory and life-changing information in this series. The wisdom shared in this book will help you to understand how to navigate through the many seasons that you'll enter and how to not do what most believers do, and that is—climax in the wrong seasons! Additionally, you will learn how to finally end your relationship with the spirit of bondage so that you can finally be who God designed you to be!

TABLE OF CONTENTS

THE POWER AND THE PURPOSE OF BOUNDARIES

It was early 2014 and I had been having a series of dreams. I'm not a big dreamer, but whenever I do dream, my dreams are oftentimes very detailed and significant. Let's look at two of the more significant ones.

Dream Number One

I had been kidnapped and I was in the custody of three people—a very aggressive woman, an aggressive man and what I believed to be their adult son, who happened to be relatively passive, but evil. In the dream, I had been forced into a relationship with the son; I somehow knew that he was my boyfriend and the three had been holding me hostage. The woman was the most aggressive of the three; she was in full control and the two men were afraid of her, even though the other guy who I believed to be her husband was also aggressive. He just wasn't as aggressive as she was.

I don't remember the entirety of everything that happened in the dream (no, there was no sex), but what I do remember is that I was terrified of the woman. She was extremely hateful and bitter, and both her and her husband had pretty much locked me in a bedroom with their son. Thankfully, he didn't touch me. He was evil; I could sense it, but he was also fearful. The woman called her son out of the room, and a few

1

minutes later, her husband entered. He sat on the bed next to me and demanded that I remove my clothes. I was horrified. What if his wife walked into the room? She'd surely accuse me of coming after her husband and I wanted nothing to do with him! Nevertheless, I was scared of him, so I started pulling down the straps on my shirt. That's when the bedroom's door opened, and the woman walked in. I felt sheer terror as she looked at us. But she didn't address the matter; instead, she started talking about something else totally unrelated (I don't remember what), and then, her husband followed her out of the room. A few minutes later, I heard a very loud sound, and somehow, I knew that I was being rescued. I believe the sound was the sound of horses; there was an army approaching the place. The son got up and left the room to see what was going on. After this, it was almost as if I was lifted up and removed from that room. Immediately, I found myself in the living room, but not standing on the floor. Instead, whatever force was carrying me allowed me to see it coming down on the woman from God's vantage point. I could see her eyes; they were filled with terror. She let out a loud, guttural scream as this force pounced on her, and from there, I felt peace—immense, immeasurable peace. And I knew I had been rescued; I knew I had been delivered.

Dream Number Two

Dream number two came a few days or maybe a few weeks after the first dream. I just remember that they were in the same time-frame. This dream was a beautiful picture of the aftermath of deliverance. In the dream, I was sitting on a bed and there was a woman in front of me putting makeup on my face. I knew that she was getting me ready for something, but for what? I remember hoping that she was doing my makeup the right way, after all, I'm used to doing my own makeup. It was almost as if she could hear my thoughts and sense my distrust. She immediately grabbed a floor mirror and placed it in front of me. I could see my reflection and I was beyond beautiful! I was at my desired weight, my makeup was perfect and my hair looked amazing! I'd never worn my hair like that, even till this day! She'd swept it all to one side and curled it, allowing my hair to flow down the side of my face onto my shoulder. And what's even more amazing is—I was wearing a wedding gown! My waistline was pretty much nonexistent! I was taken aback by how beautiful I looked, and that's when I heard a noise in the hall. I got up and went to the door to see where the noise was coming from. I saw what appeared to be a teenage girl and two pre-teen boys, and somehow, I knew that they were evil. All the same, I knew that they couldn't come into the room that I was in. They passed by the door and the girl looked at me. I think she even rolled her eyes. As they walked up ahead, the girl looked back at me, but she instinctively kept walking. Inside the room, I felt peace, joy and love. Inside that room, I finally felt safe.

Understanding the Dreams

Kidnapping is the crossing of a boundary. Anytime you override the will of another human being (minus the children under your care), you are operating in witchcraft, after all, that's all witchcraft is. It is the invoking of dark forces to aid in the destruction or manipulation of someone's will. God is our Creator and even He doesn't control us. He gives us the ability to make right and wrong choices; He gives us the ability to choose Him or choose darkness. This is why Matthew 5:37 says, "Let what you say be simply 'Yes' or 'No'; anything more than this comes from evil." In other words, don't be manipulative; be direct and straightforward. Any other mode of communication is evil; this includes being passive-aggressive and sending out subliminal messages on social media. There are three directions of communication.

1. You can talk "at" someone.
2. You can talk "to" someone.
3. You can talk "about" someone.

Taking at or about a person is evil because God wants us to communicate with one another. This is how we take away Satan's opportunity to sow discord among us. God tells us to be direct; the Bible says that the righteous are as bold as a lion (see Proverbs 28:1).

The three people in the first dream were demonic spirits; the woman represented the strongman because she was the one in control; both men were in subjection to her. Her husband came into the room and demanded that I take my clothes off; this was the generational spirit of adultery that was on my family. Her son was passive; he represented the spirit of fear. This dream represented deliverance, but before

I came out of the enemy's snare, I had to see everything that had once held me captive. This way, I could identify those spirits should they attempt to return. Of course, the rescue represented my deliverance. I was taken up and God allowed me to see this deliverance from His vantage point.

As for the second dream, I was getting dolled up for a wedding where I was the bride. This dream was two-fold. For one, it represented the Church. God was preparing His bride, and the gates of hell (the three children in the hall) would not be able to prevail against us. Next, it was a picture of the deliverance I'd undergone. The wedding dress signified me stepping into my purpose, not just as an individual, but as a member of the Church. At the same time, the woman was readying me for my new role, but my trust issues got in the way. Thankfully, they didn't halt the process, but the conversation I had in my mind about her being unable to prepare me the way I'd been preparing myself meant that, while I was getting ready, I wasn't necessarily ready for the assignment God has given me. Don't get me wrong—He was using me then just as He uses me now, but this is just a snippet of what He plans to do with and through me. In the dream, the woman could hear my innermost thoughts, so she grabbed a mirror and placed it in front of me. She wasn't angry, nor was she rude. She simply wanted to redirect my thoughts. She wanted me to trust her, and when I saw what she'd done, I was in utter awe. She'd dolled me up far better than I had ever done myself! The reflection of me was futuristic; it was a picture of my tomorrow, even though the snapshot was taken since before the establishment of time. And finally, I heard a noise and I went to go and investigate. I looked out into the hall and saw a teenage girl and two young boys. The girl appeared to be around 11 or 12 years old, so she was more of a preteen. The boys weren't too much younger than she was. I believe they represented the devils from the first dream. They'd lost their rank and power against me, just as they'd lost their access to me. This is why they were so small and so young. They couldn't come into the room that I was in; all they could do was pass me by. What had once been two and a half very intimidating devils were now measly imps or, at least, in my sight. Maybe, I'd been upgraded in rank. Either way, they couldn't get to me. "Never think the devil will walk past an open door. No! If he sees an opportunity, he's going to take it!" These are the words of my former mentor, and he had been somewhat right, but in this dream, the door to the room I was in had been open and those devils had no choice but to pass it by. In the context he'd given that revelation, he'd been one hundred percent right, after all, he was talking about an opportunity. He was essentially saying that if you give the devil an inch, he will take a mile. But that dream taught me something else. There are some rooms that neither Satan nor his henchmen can enter. These rooms are called "the will of God," and as long as we're there, Satan is powerless against us!

But why was I having dreams about bondage and freedom? In all truth, my family had been bound for generations. I wasn't just dealing with voids created by trauma, I was also dealing with voids that had not been filled with information (knowledge, wisdom) generation after generation! And understand this—a void represents darkness. This is where devils dwell. The more I came into the truth of Jesus Christ, the more those voids began to be filled with His Word, His presence and His healing power. In other words, the enemy kept losing ground! He'd once advanced against my family generation after generation, but God saw fit to end Satan's reign in my life. I should have and could have been dead or crazy, but God kept me throughout it all! The only boundaries I understood were the ones I'd put in place, and even for them, I didn't fully enforce them. When I started creating and enforcing boundaries in my life, I was still relatively young in the faith. Those boundaries drove the majority of my family out of my life because many of them don't understand or respect boundaries; they rebel against laws and boundaries, and they think that anyone who abides by them is "weak." For everyone who has clear and defined boundaries, they normally say, "They think they're better than us!" or "What goes up must come down!"

I often use snippets of my story because I am a picture of revival. I am the evidence of what God can and will do if allowed. He delivered me, not just from Satan, but He delivered me from myself! However, this deliverance wasn't anything like you'd see on the big screen. No, God requires that you be a willing and active participant in your own deliverance. This is why so many people fail to get free.

They think that by crying, threatening to commit suicide, attempting to commit suicide or turning to other gods that they'll force YAHWEH to move on their behalves. I thought that way as well. I can truly say I've thrown quite a few tantrums in the presence of God, but being the great and amazing Father He is, He completely ignored me. He let me cry, scream, rebel and do whatever I felt I needed to do to get His attention. I've had outright tantrums, tantrums disguised as prayers and passive-aggressive tantrums, none of which moved God.

Note: In most cases when a woman dreams that she's getting married, the dream is not a good one. It can signify the marriage between her and a spirit husband. Nevertheless, the dream I'd had wasn't demonic; it was a picture of the aftermath of deliverance—the exiting of one season to enter another. If you ever dream about getting married, please seek wise counsel, especially from someone who understands deliverance. Also, be sure to pray about it.

Ouch: When Boundaries are Broken

"He that diggeth a pit shall fall into it; and whoso breaketh an hedge, a serpent shall bite him" (Ecclesiastes 10:8). Behind every boundary, there is an ouch that's waiting to be said, whether it's a physical boundary, a sexual boundary, a spiritual boundary or a social boundary. If you cross a boundary that you have not been cleared to cross, you will experience some type of pain or strain, whether it be financial, physical, mental, spiritual or social. For example, I was nine-years old when mother nature taught me a very valuable lesson. I'd caught an adorable black and white kitten that had been running around our neighborhood and I'd asked my mother if I could keep the kitten. She said no, so I asked my father. He said yes. Now, my parents should have disciplined me for doing that, but they didn't. Nevertheless, I learned the hard way that wherever and whenever your parents don't discipline you, life will. And life is far more merciless than our parents can even think or imagine to be! Somewhere between a few days to a week later, I came across another kitten that was obviously the sibling of the kitten I'd originally caught. It was an orange and white tabby, and I just had to have it! It was running across the yard with my kitten running beside it (I wasn't allowed to keep my kitten in the house initially). I knew I wouldn't have any trouble catching Jinro (my cat) because he trusted me, but the other kitten would be a challenge to keep. Howbeit, I was willing and ready to take on that challenge, so I went directly to my dad and asked him if I could keep the second kitten if I caught it. He said yes like I knew he would.

The next day, I spotted the kittens running together. My brother and I tried to catch the orange kitten, but it ran towards our backyard with Jinro in tow. Finally, the kittens came to a boundary. They came to a gate that separated our backyard from our adjacent neighbor's backyard. We knew that we weren't supposed to go in that yard (we'd been warned), but when the kittens went through the gate to get away from us, neither of us could resist climbing the fence. I was the more athletic one, so I jumped the gate first and my brother followed suit. The kittens ran across the backyard towards a huge bush. The kittens stopped and looked at me before running into the bush, but I kept walking towards them. My brother, on the other hand, kept his distance. He'd stopped halfway across the yard, and from there, he'd decided to be a spectator. I rushed up to the bush and pulled back one of the branches. That's when I heard buzzing noises. When I looked up, I saw a huge beehive and a bunch of what looked like carpenter bees. I panicked and let the branch go, causing it to snap into place, possibly disturbing or dislodging the hive. I started running back towards the part of the gate that I'd jumped over, but it was too late. I felt the first sting, then the second and then, the third. Before long, my little body was riddled with bees and bee stings, but I kept running with all of my might. Of course, my brother had already taken off and escaped the wrath of the bees. I threw my body across the gate, scraping my stomach on the way over. The metal from the gate ripped into my skin, but I was too distracted by all the bees to even feel the cut initially. I finally got far enough away so the bees stopped attacking me, but I remember that I had more than 13 stings on my body that we could count. As I approached the house, I was met by my brother who, of course, thought the whole incident was funny. I was limping as I made my way towards the front door of our house. After we got inside, my brother called my mother at work, but by this time, I'd already started lying down after having looked at a few of my wounds. I don't remember if I pulled any stings out; I just remember feeling extremely drowsy and lying down. I'm not sure if that was the effect of the stings. Honestly, I don't remember if he'd called her before I'd gone to sleep or while I was asleep. I just remember him handing me the phone. Of course, my mother did what most Southern mothers did back in those days. She fussed at me and told me to just lie down.

Our skin is a boundary. The primary function of the skin is to act as a barrier and a protective covering. That day, my skin was broken more than once. That day, I probably said "Ouch" more times than I've ever said that word in my life! Now, I could have sat there and blamed it on the bees, after all, this is what most of society does. I could have blamed the fence for scratching my belly. I could have blamed my brother for trying to save himself in the middle of a chaotic event. I could have even blamed my parents for leaving us at home while they went to work. This is how most people become bitter. They fail to see their role in their own pain, therefore, they point the fingers of blame at everybody but themselves. Consequently, they spend the majority of their lives screaming out in pain and pointing their fingers at everyone else but themselves. Howbeit, it was my own fault. First, I knew I wasn't supposed to be in the neighbor's backyard. Next, my mother had made it painfully clear that she didn't want any pets except the goldfish we had in the house. But I'd manipulated the situation by asking my father, and then, I continued pressing the boundaries of my mother's patience by going after a second kitten. In short, it was all my fault. I remember the incident vividly, but I've never held anyone at fault for it but myself. I understood that I was wrong, and because I understood this, I didn't receive any psychological scars from the event (except a fear of and respect for bees and their counterparts). Nowadays, it's just a funny memory that I share with people. I use that story to teach a very valuable lesson, and that is—wherever your parents fail to discipline you, life will. In short, I was able to move beyond the event because I took accountability for it, even at the age of nine.

The purpose of boundaries is to protect, not only you, but to protect the systems that God created. The purpose of man's boundaries is to protect the systems that we've created. Think about a stop sign. It serves as a boundary. You may be able to run it a few times without consequence, but if you keep running it, you'll eventually hit someone, be hit by someone or you'll receive a traffic citation. Stop signs are a part of what we call our traffic system. They play an intricate part in reducing the amount of car-related accidents and fatalities. Amazingly enough, we are surrounded by systems, all of which are designed to work together to ensure the safety, sanity, productivity, creativity and prosperity of every system put in place to protect and prosper us. Think about the camera on your phone. It's a part of a larger system. First, there's a system that allows the camera to take pictures and record videos. Next, there's a feature that allows your camera's system to partner with other programs so that you can edit and upgrade your photos and videos on the worldwide web. Instagram has its own system, but Instagram had to create another system that would allow it to encode and upload whatever you produced with your camera, and it doesn't end there. They needed another system that would allow them to host your video and photo content. This is called a server. Developers put together these systems, and they have to work independently before they can work interdependently; this is to ensure that these systems can benefit from one another. And, of course, each system has boundaries. What hackers do is try to decode the programs' codes so that they can access sensitive information and hijack those systems. This is why there are several types of boundaries put in place to protect them. The first one is antivirus software. Another one is called our legal system. While hacking within itself is not yet recognized as a crime, most hackers commit crimes whenever they hack someone's computer without their consent or when they steal sensitive information or intellectual property. When these boundaries are broken, the first line of defense is the firewall, and next, the antivirus software. The program developers will work together with law enforcement to help bring the hacker or hackers to justice. Again, behind every boundary there's an ouch waiting to be said and a tear that's waiting to be shed. Think about the many times when you crossed a boundary that you shouldn't have crossed. What happened as a result of that?

I was around 15-years old, and I had gone to stay with some of my cousins for the summer. One of my cousins had a one-year old baby boy who, like most toddlers, wanted to get into everything. One day, I was curling my hair and he was standing next to me. After I would finish a curl, I would put the curling iron down on the dresser and grab the feather comb I had been using. The problem was that every time I put the curling iron down, my cousin's son would stand on his tiptoes and try to reach for the device. "No, no! Hot!" I said this several times, but every time I put the curling iron down, he would reach past my "no" and try to grab it. Finally, my cousin (who happened to be in the bathroom doing her hair) yelled out at me. She told me to stop telling him no and just let him grab the curling iron. I thought she was the worst mother in the world at that moment, so I didn't listen. A few minutes later, I found myself saying it again. "No, no! Hot! No, no! Hot!" I heard a slamming noise coming from the bathroom. My cousin screamed out again, but this time, she was angry. "Stop yelling at him! How is he supposed to know what hot is if you don't let him touch it?!" (Or something to that effect). It made sense, but he was still a toddler. After being yelled at one or two more times, I finally gave in. I watched him stand on his tiptoes and blindly reach onto the dresser, trying to grab the curling iron. I cringed as his little hand got closer to the metal, but I had to honor his mother's request. Finally, he made contact with the curling iron, and he didn't just barely touch it; he was moving so fast that he wrapped his hand around the metal. Of course, he withdrew that hand faster than he'd extended it. He screamed and immediately began to cry. "Hot, hot!" I shouted once again, wondering if I'd just scarred the child for life. But as cruel as this event seemed, it probably saved his life. After that incident, any time we said, "Hot, hot," he would withdraw his hand and repeat what we'd said. Behind every boundary, there is an ouch. And that rambunctious and curious toddler discovered this truth on that particular day.

The same is true for you. Every time you've cried about a person you shouldn't have dated, you are experiencing the effects of a violated boundary. Think about how your body responds whenever your skin has been cut. The following information was taken from Science Focus:

"When the skin is punctured, blood vessels contract and platelets release fibrin proteins that tangle together to form a clot and seal the wound. Next the blood vessels expand again to allow white blood cells to flock to the wound site. These attack any bacteria that got past the clot.

(Source: Science Focus/What Happens in My Body When I Get a Cut?)

Tears, like blood, are oftentimes the result of a violated or a crossed boundary. Remember that, as humans, we are living souls; we are spirits locked in a structure called a body. The soul is comprised of three dimensions; they are the conscious mind, subconscious mind and unconscious mind. The conscious mind is what we readily engage at any given time. As you're reading this book, your conscious mind is being engaged. Your conscious represents your present awareness. It also stores information that you have not yet rendered to be true or false. Again, it is the waiting room of

15

the soul. The subconscious mind, on the other hand, is the heart. This is what God told us to guard. This is the epicenter or control center of our soul. This is the part of us that Satan passionately desires to enter. How does he enter the subconscious? Through belief. Every string of information sitting in the conscious mind is waiting on its time to be examined. Most of it will never be examined, so it'll expire in the waiting room. This includes the scriptures that we read! When information enters the waiting room, it serves as knowledge, but once it enters the heart or the subconscious, it is broken down until it becomes understanding. Anytime information in the conscious is approved for the subconscious, we experience anything from shock to joy to grief; this is because we are believing whatever it is that we've allowed in. But whenever that information is ungodly or false, we often experience anything from offense to fear to grief to anxiety. These are all alarms that have been set off. Our soul responds to this event by changing the temperature of our emotions. Consequently, we may start crying, yelling or panicking. For example, I've had plenty of people to tell me that they are afraid to advance in God because they believe that if they continue pursuing Him that the devil is going to kill them. This is a lie from the pits of hell. Howbeit, what has happened here is the enemy tossed a dart at them; the dart is a lie. It went from their conscious to their subconscious, and whenever this happened, they found themselves dealing with persistent thoughts of death and demonic retaliation. And of course, once the enemy successfully entered their subconscious, they found themselves in need of deliverance, and the evidence of this was the repeated and ever-growing fear of wholeheartedly surrendering to God. Consequently, the experienced moments when they were afraid to get behind the wheels of their cars or do anything they felt would put them at greater risk. This was the evidence that the boundary between their conscious mind and their subconscious mind had been penetrated and the enemy was now on the wrong side of that boundary. This is why the Bible tells us to cast down evil imaginations and every high thing that exalts itself against the knowledge of God and bring into captivity every thought to the obedience of Christ.

On the other side of the pain spectrum is pleasure. This is what we all want. We all want to be happy; we all want to experience Heaven on Earth. And the human experience can be summed up as us constantly going through hours, days, weeks, months and years of discomfort, pain and frustration just to reap and enjoy a few moments of pleasure and peace. Think about it—we wake up extra early so that we can decorate ourselves for wherever it is that we're heading to; this is so that we can be visually appealing to others. Why? Because we've come to believe that if people like what they see, they'll extend favor and grace to us. When we're married, we endure the worst sides of our spouses just so that we can enjoy a few moments with their good sides. We endure them at their worst so that we can experience them at their best. (Note: the average couple has sex 54 times a year; that's once a week. Studies show that the average sexual encounter between couples is 5.44 minutes to twenty minutes, all the way up to 44 minutes. There are 168 hours in a week. This means that if a couple has a single sexual encounter with his or her spouse for 44 minutes in a week's time, that couple has sex less than one percent of the time they're married. Why is this important? Because a lot of believers get married just so they can have legal, God-approved sex! So, if your relationship is built on lust, your marriage is already on unstable grounds!) All the same, consider our children. We spend and invest in them, tolerating all the noise, destruction and every headache that comes with raising them; this is just so that we can eventually see them grow up and become Godly, loving, healthy and successful adults! We work eight hours a day (on average) for five days out of the week, tolerating narcissistic, condescending and competitive co-workers. This is so that we can then turn around and give most of the money that we've earned away to our bill collectors. We then take a little of what we have left and try to do something nice for ourselves. We're paying for our homes so that we'll have a roof over our heads; we're paying our utilities so that we can be comfortable. We toil just so that we can enjoy the fruits of our labor! We endure the pain so that we can get to the pleasure. But before we endure the painful and expensive journey of building anything from a business to a family, we must count the costs. For example, as an entrepreneur, I only sow where I know or believe that I'll get a return on my investment. I created a couple of black and gold logos at one point and it took them years to sell from my

store. What I learned was that as pretty as those colors are together, there is absolutely no demand for black and gold logos in the world of ministry. What this meant for me was that I had to stop investing time or resources into developing black and gold designs. If I continued doing so, I would have lessened the value of my business and the amount of profits that I could potentially earn from that business.
Consequently, I would have no one to blame for this but myself. The point is—invest! This is what builders do, but when you realize that you're throwing money, time, tears and sweat into a bottomless pit, count your losses and move on! A good businessman or woman knows when to cut his or her losses! As a matter of fact, entrepreneurship is an expensive lesson that consists of the entrepreneur spending eighty to ninety percent of his or her time and resources learning a bunch of hard lessons, and then reaping a small to great reward. When a business begins to turn a substantial profit, please know that the owner is only getting back a tenth of what he or she invested! Remember, not all investments are monetary; the most valuable asset that we all have is our time! The point is that boundaries are necessary for us to enjoy all the good that life has to offer, but when the boundaries between two worlds are crossed, pain is inevitable. This includes the membrane or the boundary between two seasons. The pain associated with leaving one season to enter another can be almost unbearable. This is why most people get to the edge of their breakthroughs and give up. But breakthrough feels how it sounds; it feels like something breaking through our skin. It can be painful and

uncomfortable, but it's necessary! It also affords us the lives and the lifestyles that we've dreamed of. The older generation used to say it this way, "No pain, no gain."

THE PERIOD AT THE END OF A SENTENCE

The following story was taken from Wikipedia.com:

"On July 31st, 2009, three Americans, Joshua Fattal, Sarah Shourd and Shane Bauer were taken into custody by Iranian border guards for crossing into Iran while hiking near the Iranian border in Iraqi Kurdistan. At the time of their detention by Iranian troops, the three Americans were on vacation from their jobs in the region in a relatively stable, autonomous region of Iraq known as Iraqi Kurdistan. On the recommendations of locals, they hiked to see a popular local Iraqi tourist destination near the Iraq-Iran border, the Ahmed Awa waterfall.

Following the hikers' capture on the Iraqi-Iranian border, a wide range of outside voices, including the Secretary-General of the United Nations, Ban Ki-moon, and the human rights group Amnesty International, had called for the hikers' unconditional release. Iran subsequently claimed the three were spies but offered no evidence to support its contention.

Sarah Shourd was released 14 months later on 'humanitarian grounds'. Fattal and Bauer were convicted of 'illegal entry' and 'espionage' two years after their arrest and each sentenced to eight years in prison, but were released on September 21, 2011. Each of the detainees was released after payment of 5 billion rials (about US$465,000) bail was arranged by the Sultan of Oman."

(Reference: Wikipedia.com/2009–11 Detention of American Hikers by Iran)

Have you ever heard the phrase, "A thin line?" Of course, you have! It simply denotes that there is a thread of difference between two realities or systems. For example, people often say that there's a thin line between love and hate. Let me be the first to tell you that this is a lie! On the spectrum of love versus hatred, tolerance would be at the center. Love and hate are as far apart as Heaven is from hell. God is love (period). That settles it, even though for the human mind, this saying within itself, while poetic, is a complete mystery. How can God be love when we've been taught that love is an emotion? We've been taught that love is a feeling that overshadows us and makes us do stupid things. That's not love. It's called dopamine. Also referred to as a "chemical messenger," dopamine acts as both a hormone and a neurotransmitter. Amazingly enough, scientists say that dopamine has the same effect on the brain as cocaine. "Be sober, be vigilant; because your adversary the devil, as a roaring lion, walketh about, seeking whom he may devour" (1 Peter 5:8).

Joshua Fattal, Sarah Shourd and Shane Bauer discovered what a "thin line" was the day they decided to tread on the border that separated Iraq from Iran. Remember, anytime you illegally cross a boundary, you will find yourself bound! This is what happened to this trio. They unknowingly crossed a boundary and it cost them dearly! Sarah Shourd served 14 months in prison; the men on the other hand served two years, one month and 21 days in prison! If this is what happens in the natural, can you imagine what happens in the spirit realm when we illegally cross boundaries?! Yes, even boundaries we didn't realize were illegal! For example, at the age of 17, I didn't know that messing with an Ouija board was wrong, but this did not exempt me from its effects! God said it this way, "My people are destroyed for lack of knowledge. Because you have rejected knowledge, I also will reject you from being priests for Me; because you have forgotten the law of your God, I also will forget your children." In short, what you don't know can kill you after all! Ignorance is a serious crime in the Kingdom because you don't have to be ignorant, after all, information is all around you! Now, God gives us grace; that is the space and the opportunity to learn, but if we abuse it, we can step across its boundaries into God's mercy. Mercy, for me, makes me think of a twisted game my brother and I used to play (ironically called Mercy). We would bend each others' middle fingers back as far as we could. The person who could take the most pain was considered the winner. First, he'd start with me since I was always losing. He'd bend my finger and I'd try to take the pain as much as I could. A few seconds in, I'd scream, "Mercy!" Then, it was my turn. I would try to bend my brother's finger back as far as I could, and I would do this until he screamed, "Mercy!" Another rendition of this game was someone twisting one of your arms behind your back until the pain became unbearable.

- Grace looks like Joshua Fattal, Sarah Shourd and Shane Bauer walking over the border; it was the space of time they had to acknowledge that uncomfortable feeling that told them that they were out of place.
- Mercy looks like Joshua Fattal and Shane Bauer being sentenced to eight years, but serving two years.

The time that this duo spent in prison is what we call a sentence. What's amazing is, we all understand sentencing as it relates to our judicial system, but we don't necessarily understand it as it relates to our lives. Let me ask you this question—how many years did you serve in that last relationship of yours? Believe it or not, that's called a sentence! Sentences can sometimes be self-inflicted. The five types of sentences are:

1. God-inflicted
2. Sin-inflicted
3. Satan-inflicted
4. Self-inflicted
5. Man-inflicted

God-inflicted: We see an example of this type of sentence with Zechariah. He'd received a visitation from the angel of the Lord, Gabriel, and Gabriel told Zechariah that his wife, Elizabeth, would bear him a son named John. The angel also spoke of John's assignment in the Earth, but after having a dramatic display of religiousness (Zechariah had fallen on the angel when he'd seen him), the man of God failed the test of faith. He'd been performing in the temple (he was a priest), but when the moment came for his faith to be tested, he'd failed. Luke 1:18-20 (ESV) details the rest of this story. "And Zechariah said to the angel, 'How shall I know this? For I am an old man, and my wife is advanced in years.' And the angel answered him, 'I am Gabriel. I stand in the presence of God, and I was sent to speak to you and to bring you this good news. And behold, you will be silent and unable to speak until the day that these things take place, because you did not believe my words, which will be fulfilled in their time.'" This is an example of a God-inflicted sentence. Another well-known example of a God-inflicted sentence is the one He'd given to the Israelites after they'd murmured and complained in the wilderness. Numbers 32:6-13 (ESV) says, "And Moses said unto the children of Gad and to the children of Reuben, Shall your brethren go to war, and shall ye sit here? And wherefore discourage ye the heart of the children of Israel from going over into the land which the LORD hath given them? Thus did your fathers, when I sent them from Kadeshbarnea to see the land. For when they went up unto the valley of Eshcol, and saw the land, they discouraged the heart of the children of Israel, that they should not go into the land which the LORD had given them. And the LORD'S anger was kindled the same time, and he swear, saying, Surely none of the men that came up out of Egypt, from twenty years old and upward, shall see the land which I swear unto Abraham, unto Isaac, and unto Jacob; because they have not wholly followed me: Save Caleb the son of Jephunneh the Kenezite, and Joshua the son of Nun: for they have wholly followed the LORD. And the LORD'S anger was kindled against Israel, and he made them wander in the wilderness forty years, until all the generation, that had done evil in the sight of the LORD, was consumed." This sentence is what we call a generational curse.

In truth, many of us have served time under God-inflicted sentences. For example, you may have wanted to get away from that narcissist you were dating, but for whatever reason, you could not seem to let go. God warned you through His Word and His people about that relationship, but you did not listen. You cut off anyone and everyone who dared to tell you the hard truth, and after giving enough sacrificial offerings, you secured your relationship with that person at the expense of your sanity. In other words, your attempt to secure that relationship eventually caused you to become insecure. You may have even married the person. Consequently, you went through some of the greatest storms while in that marriage. You turned to the left; there was no one around to help you. You turned to the right; there was no one around to help you. You took advice from the enemy, but it only seemed to add years to your sentence. And finally, you looked up. You prayed without ceasing, but God seemed to respond to every prayer except the prayer about your relationship. They laid hands on you in church, and you passed out under the power of God, only to have to get back up and go back home to the weapon that had been formed against you. You tried everything, and finally, you repented—you truly repented, and not that religious, "I'm sorry" that most folks dust off and throw at God. You acknowledged your wrong and took full responsibility for your actions. And finally, after five-years of romantic slavery, the way of escape finally reopened itself. This small window in time opened a portal that allowed you to legally run for your life. Maybe, your spouse or insignificant other cheated. Maybe, your spouse hit you. This time, you jumped out that window with your hands lifted, shouting, "Lord, I surrender!" Whatever it is that he or she did proved to be a rescue attempt on God's part, allowing you to start recovering the shattered pieces of your soul. You had been sentenced to five-years with your idol; this way, God could prove to you that the man of your dreams or the woman of your dreams did not have the tools, the information, the capacity or the love needed to fix that God-sized hole in your heart! He used that sentence to deliver you from idolatry!

Sin-inflicted: This is similar to a God-inflicted sentence, but the difference is, it's not personal! When God sentences a person, for example, to three years in a relationship that he or she chose for himself or herself, and several years of mental recovery, it's normally because that person has a call on his or her life. That person has an assignment, but he or she keeps being irresponsible with his or her soul and distracted by the things of this world. To burn out this residue, God will oftentimes give people what they think they want. So, if marriage is your idol and you keep engaging in sexual immorality in an attempt to speed up the plans of God or to hijack God's will for your life, it is possible that He will allow you to get married in the region of thought that you're in. Keep in mind that the only people who will pursue you romantically in that region of thought are just as idolatrous and perverted as you are, if not more. It doesn't matter what titles they have or how anointed they are, if they meet and marry you in your perversion, it's only because they live in the neighborhood of your thinking. God knows that by allowing you to have what you think you want, you will soon discover that it's nothing like you imagined it to be. It's hard to be married to broken people, especially when you yourself are broken. He knows what it will take to bring you to your knees in repentance. Again, these are God-inflicted boundaries, but sin-inflicted boundaries are boundaries created when God gave us, the body of Christ, instructions. For example, we are no longer under the Mosaic Law; that was our former region of thought. We are now under the dispensation of grace, but this DOES NOT mean that we are free to do as we please! No! We are BOUND to do as we please, but we are FREE to do what pleases Him! We are still servants of Jesus Christ! Please understand that it is still a sin to murder your brother and it is still a sin to dishonor your parents! Fornication is STILL a sin! But these sins fall under one category—the absence of love! That is, not loving God with all of your heart, soul and mind, and not loving your neighbor as you love yourself (see Matthew 22:37). Fornication also falls under the absence of faith (see

Romans 14:23). But the dispensation of grace simply means that you live in a space where you can no longer be stoned to death or cast out of the camp should you or, better yet, when you miss the mark. It also means that Jesus paid the price for you! Nowadays, you have grace (space and time) to repent! Apostle Paul said, "Let not sin therefore reign in your mortal body, that ye should obey it in the lusts thereof. Neither yield ye your members as instruments of unrighteousness unto sin: but yield yourselves unto God, as those that are alive from the dead, and your members as instruments of righteousness unto God. For sin shall not have dominion over you: for ye are not under the law, but under grace. What then? Shall we sin, because we are not under the law, but under grace? God forbid. Know ye not, that to whom ye yield yourselves servants to obey, his servants ye are to whom ye obey; whether of sin unto death, or of obedience unto righteousness?" (Romans 6:12-16). And the amazing part is, this has absolutely nothing to do with works! Faith without works is dead; we know this! But did you know that you actually do have faith? Sometimes, it's just misplaced, meaning, you may have faith in the wrong things or the wrong people.

Sin-inflicted sentences are the result of you going outside of God's will for your life simply because:
1. You want something.
2. You don't trust God to give you what you want.
3. You're not patient enough to wait on God.
4. What you want may be outside of God's camp (will)

for you.

Consequently, people who go past these boundaries end up bound simply because they crossed over into enemy territory. Think about Joshua Fattal, Sarah Shourd and Shane Bauer. They were legally in Iraq, but they illegally crossed the border into Iran. If you go into sin looking for a blessing, you have entered into the enemy's territory, and while God may extend His grace to you, if you don't take that opportunity to repent, God's mercy will have to meet you there. This is because the Bible tells us to "give no place to the devil." The word "place" in this text means opportunity! The Bible also tells us that Satan, like a roaring lion, walks around, seeking whom he may devour. The keyword here is "may," meaning, he needs an opportunity. Imagine it this way—the will of God is a country and Sin is another country. The will of God represents the love of God; it represents holiness and selflessness. The will of God is one region of thought, but sin is another region of thought. You're in the will of God, but just a few feet over the border into Sin, you see a bushel of blackberries. They look sweet and ripe. The more you look at them, the more an appetite for those berries form in your mind. You step over the boundary just a hair and retrieve a blackberry. The blackberry would dissipate in the will of God, so you have to eat it in Sin; you have to eat it in the darkness of doubt and offense before stepping back into the will of God. You eat the blackberry, and just as you suspected, it is better than delicious! It's like nothing you've ever tried before! After you're done, you rush back into God's will, and you try to wash the residue of Sin off you so no one will know what you've been up to. That blackberry is filling for that particular moment, so you stay in the will of God for a few more days. Unbeknownst to you, it has created a void in your soul; this void serves as a belly, and that belly has an appetite! It begins to crave and demand more of those blackberries! A week later, you're treading on that border again, and you see another bushel of blackberries, but this time, they are even bigger than the ones you saw last week. They look juicier and sweeter, but the problem is, you'd have to go just a little further into Sin to get to them. Last week, you were able to slightly step over the border, but this time, you'll have to go a little deeper into Sin to get the blackberry. You look both ways, and when no one is looking, you run over the line and grab another blackberry. Again, you have to eat it in darkness, so you have to eat it in Sin before rushing back into the will of God. These blackberries are bigger, so it takes you a little longer to consume the one you picked. You watch the window of escape as it gets smaller and smaller, and just in the nick of time, you're able to jump through that window, dust yourself off and apologize to God yet again. Three days later, it happens again. You see a bushel of blackberries and some raspberries over in Sin, and they are ginormous! You're more comfortable with crossing that border now because you're slowly becoming desensitized to sin, so you rush over into Sin and grab a raspberry. This time, you don't care who sees you. This time, you've reasoned with yourself that everybody in the church is a hypocrite, therefore, they all must be doing what you're doing, so your heart towards the church begins to grow more and more bitter. At the same time, what you find in Sin seems to taste sweeter. And this time, you have to go even further into Sin to get what you want. While eating the raspberry, you keep watching that small window called grace, and you know that you can make it through it so you shove the rest of the raspberry into your mouth before grabbing a blackberry. The blackberry is so sinfully sweet that you lose track of time trying to savor it. When you look up, the window is a few seconds away from closing, but you're so far into Sin that it's nearly impossible for you to make it. Nevertheless, you run towards that window as fast as you can. You leap, and you're about to make it, but all of a sudden, something grabs your right foot. Before you look down, you remember something God said to Satan in the Garden of Eden. In Genesis 3:15, He said, "I will put enmity between you and the woman, and between your offspring and her offspring; he shall bruise your head, and you shall bruise his heel." You look down, and sure enough, it's that ole serpent, Satan, holding onto your foot. You plead with him to let you go, but he doesn't respond. He just laughs mercilessly as if he can't hear you. You then begin to call on the name of the Lord, and somehow, Satan looses your foot and you're able to jump through that window just in time. The Lord has saved you from yourself. He rebukes you in love and tells you not to go back into Sin. He says to you, "Go and sin no more" or, better yet, "Go in Sin no more." With gratitude in your heart, shame on your face and blueberry juice around your mouth, you nod your head in agreement.

"Yes sir," you say as the tears flow down your face. "This time, I'm living for you, Lord. No more Sin!" Months go by, and you've been doing great! You've stayed away from Sin, you've written a book about Sin and you have met what appears to be the love of your life. One day, you're talking with your new boyfriend (girlfriend, if you're a man) about the berries you had in Sin. He sounds extremely interested. As a matter of fact, he's had his own experiences in Sin. "Have you tried the strawberries over there?!" he asks with passion oozing out of his tongue. "No," you counter. "But I'm sure they're good." Your boyfriend giggles. "Listen, you haven't lived until you've tried Sin's strawberries! The last time I had some, I almost let that window close on purpose! Let's go to the border tomorrow and I'll point some out to you." You agree. The next day, the two of you fool around on the borders of Sin. "Look over there!" he says, pointing across the border to some of the biggest, reddest and most plump strawberries you've ever seen! "And look, there's Deacon John," he points out. "You see, we all fall short of the glory of God! That's why He gave us grace." *In this, he's attempting to use grace as a condom, but I digress.* "Let's go all the way this time!" he says, looking you in your eyes. "We're already on the edge. Why not just go all the way?" The two of you look both ways and rush over into Sin, and this time, you have to go further than you've ever gone, but your boyfriend assures you that you'll make it back in time. He points at Deacon John, who happened to be jumping back out of Sin and into the will of God, hoping no one saw him. "He made it and so will we." Your boyfriend leads you into Sin, and the two of you start chomping away on a single strawberry, after all, the strawberries there are huge. "This is so good!" you shout. "Why don't we have strawberries like these in the will of God?" You bite down into the strawberry again, but you realize that you haven't heard anything from your boyfriend. You'd just assumed that he was enjoying the strawberry too much to speak, but when you look up, he's nowhere to be found. Your heart skips a beat before panic sets in. You look at the way of escape, but there's no way you can make it to it on time. Again, you run with all of your might towards the will of God, but the window closes, and once again, Satan grabs your foot. When you look at Satan, he looks a lot like your boyfriend. "Wait," you say. "How? I met you in church, for God's sake!" Your boyfriend snarls, "Where did you think I'd be?!" With that, you start calling on the name of the Lord again, but this time, all He says is, "My grace is sufficient for you." What does that even mean?! And why won't He rescue you, after all, we all fall short of His glory; don't we?! Satan takes you into captivity and you end up serving 15 years in that abusive relationship. In Sin, there's a hedge of protection surrounding you. Because you're a Kingdom citizen, God tells Satan that he cannot kill you, and as long as you stay within the four walls of that hedge of protection, he can't fully break you. Nevertheless, you're still in Sin, living a life contrary to the will of God. You give birth in that abyss. You buy your groceries in that place. You meet and marry another Christian in that dark place. Fifteen years later, the way of escape opens again, but this time, going through that window is going to be even more painful than staying in Sin. This is because you are now shaped like Sin, and that window will break away at you until you look like Jesus. At the same time, you count the costs and realize that you're going to lose everything of value should you reenter God's will for your life! You run and jump through that window and it hurts like hell—literally! This is what a sin-inflicted sentence looks like.

Satan-inflicted: This border narrowly meets the sin-inflicted border. This can be a generational issue that has arisen as a result of your ancestors' sins OR it is possible for God to do what He'd done with Job. Even though Job was a righteous man, God allowed Satan to test him. And while this may seem unfair to the individual who's going through the hardships, God sees a bigger picture. Job's story has benefited and inspired billions of believers. It's nothing any of us want to endure, but when we find ourselves in the furnaces of a trial, we often turn to the book of Job to encourage ourselves. I gave an example of this in Book Five about my Uncle Mannix Franklin. He'd lost his life prematurely; he'd been shot by the cops when he was just 31-years old. His son, Mannix Franklin, Jr. died 13 years later after being shot by his mother's boyfriend, and a little over three months later, his grandson, Mannix Franklin III, died while sleeping next to his mother. This tells me that one of our ancestors had been potentially playing with witchcraft. I believe this because even though it wasn't spoken of out loud, witchcraft was a common practice in the South in the early 1900's. It's not because the people were bad people;

they just didn't know any better. Whenever they faced hardships, they turned to whatever it was that they knew. And one thing about witchcraft is, whenever you play with it, you enter into a contract with the devil. Think about the border that separates God's will from sin. Witchcraft is someone crossing that border into sin and contractually agreeing to stay there for several generations in exchange for, in most cases, peace, wealth, happiness or some sort of resolve. People who play with this dark art don't know or read the small print on this contract, so they go deeper and deeper into sin until they don't know who they are anymore. Can you imagine what Satan would do if he had the green light to do everything to you that he fantasizes about doing? He'd take his time torturing you! And this is what he's done to many families who were born, not just in sin, but in the trenches, the valleys and the pits of sin. They were born in ditches and fed with lies most of their lives! This is what we call a generational curse. And many people under generational curses die, not just in sin, but as a result of it.

Self-inflicted: Proverbs 6:1-5 says, "My son, if thou be surety for thy friend, if thou hast stricken thy hand with a stranger, Thou art snared with the words of thy mouth, thou art taken with the words of thy mouth. Do this now, my son, and deliver thyself, when thou art come into the hand of thy friend; go, humble thyself, and make sure thy friend. Give not sleep to thine eyes, nor slumber to thine eyelids. Deliver thyself as a roe from the hand of the hunter, and as a bird from the hand of the fowler." One thing you'll notice is that all of these sentences are behind borders that correlate to one another. Let's have an adult conversation. You were in the middle of a "heated exchange" (sex) with your insignificant other. Your dopamine was running high in that moment, so you opened your mouth and began to ensnare your soul all the more. "It's yours forever!" you shouted. "Forever, baby! I'm yours forever!" And while you were parked on a dirt road, fogging up the windows of your lover's SUV, hell was transcribing your words onto a contract. And just like that, you were obsessed! And just like that, the way of escape closed and you found yourself being drug around in sin by a soul tie that happened to be attached to a dried-up blackberry with legs. All the same, self-inflicted sentences are not always the result of romantic relationships. The most common ones are called loans. We all run towards them. We justify getting them. And we shake hands with the banker who helped us to ensnare our souls (mind, will and emotions) because, in that moment, we're excited about being able to finally do some of the things we've been wanting to do. We crank up our new cars and drive them off the lot, thinking about every person we want to go and visit just so we can show off our shiny new wardens. Our best friends come outside and jump for joy with us, and that's when we give them the stats of our new vehicles. "It was $44,799! They gave me a five-thousand dollar discount, so the total price without taxes was $39,799. With a 4.67 percent interest rate, I'll be paying $760 a month for the next five years!" Your friend is excited because you're happy, but she's more financially responsible, so she asks, "How about insurance?" You shrug your shoulders and say, "The agent says my insurance will be $811.71, but we're looking to see if we can find something cheaper." So, for the next five years, you are a slave of that vehicle. For the next five years, you pay well over $15 hundred a month just so that you can impress a bunch of folks who don't even like you! This is what we call a self-inflicted sentence. "Owe no man any thing, but to love one another: for he that loveth another hath fulfilled the law" (Romans 13:8).

Man-inflicted: Sometimes, you may find yourself enduring sentences in regions of thought that are not entirely your fault. But the great news is, you can easily rush through a man-inflicted sentence if you don't want to be there. The bad news is, you have to overcome people-bondage, and by doing this, you just might lose some relationships. For example, some people will write you off but befriend you at the same time! Seriously! By befriending you, they (in essence) begin to introduce you to their perceptions of you. If they are able to leave the waiting room of your heart and enter into your subconscious by disguising themselves as friends, they will slowly begin to chip away at your self-esteem, all the while, planting seeds of mediocrity and inferiority in your heart. They'll discourage you when you need encouragement, they'll ignore you when everyone else is celebrating you and they'll celebrate you every time you step outside of God's will. And when you're in the pits of a storm, they'll draw closer to you because they want front-row seats to your pain. And get this, sometimes, we marry these folks; sometimes, we call them our best friends. Sometimes, we partner with them in business. Sometimes, we ask them to be the maids of honor at our weddings! Having grown up poor and broken, I soon learned how rigid people can be in their perceptions of you. Once they make up their minds about you, that's it! You would never be able to serve in any other capacity if they had their say in regards to you. For example, I remember hearing relatives talking about what they believed my future would look like. One particular story took place while I was around 13-years old, riding in the back seat of my mother's car. Another relative of ours was in the front passenger's seat. My Salt-N-Pepa cassette was in the cassette player. An intro of a young girl talking to herself came on, and before she could say much, my relative looked at my mother and said, "Now, listen to this! Every time I hear this, I think about Tiffany! This is going to be Tiffany because she's so fast!" My mother was passive. She would just ignore ill-words spoken over us, but I couldn't ignore them. The intro starts off with a 16-year old girl frantically talking to herself. She was recounting the mistake her and her boyfriend, Mario, had made by not wearing a condom. "Where is Mario?!" she screamed. "I called him over an hour ago!" Right after those words, Mario came on the scene. The two of them argued about her reason for calling him; he wanted to watch the game, but she had some bad news for him. Finally, she told him that she had tested positive for HIV. They argued about it, and of course, he accused her of sleeping around with other guys. After that, he left. And that was the gist of it. I learned pretty early in life to disconnect myself from people who had placed a period where God placed a comma regarding my future. Thankfully, those words never came to pass in my life, and they will never come to pass because they did not come from the Most High God. Around the age of 15 or 16, I started disassociating myself from a lot of my relatives. Whenever they came to visit, I stayed in my room or went over to a friend's house. I even asked my mother why she allowed her kinfolks to speak evil over her children, after all, this had become commonplace. I told her that people felt way too comfortable saying whatever they wanted to say about her children, but she couldn't speak one negative word about theirs. Again, my mother was an amazing and very kind woman; she simply said that she just ignored them when they were talking crazy. Howbeit, I could not and would not ignore them, so at the age of 15, I started drawing boundaries around myself. I started removing every relative from my life who repeatedly spoke evil about me and/or my siblings. This was just a snippet of what was to come! Even though I wasn't saved and I learned to draw boundaries through trial and error, the point is—I drew them!

People can decide that you'll never be anything, especially if you've come from nothing. We discussed cliques earlier, and let's be honest, there are some cliques that are what we call power-cliques. They were formed by people who, for one reason or another, feel entitled to success. You weren't invited into that circle because you didn't look like you'd be much or do much! You looked like you'd spend your life in mediocrity, so they were willing to accept you as a fan, but not as a co-laborer. By rejecting you, they were in their own way attempting to sentence you to whatever it was that they believed about you. The heaviest and thickest warfare you'll ever encounter will oftentimes come from these people! Ask anyone who's garnered any measure of true success! These folks won't support you, and if they find themselves in a place where they are celebrated more than you are, they will use their power and influence to degrade and devalue you! They will show others how <u>they</u> want you to be treated, even if that means ignoring you, not inviting you to any gatherings and never interacting with you besides a nod of the head or a faint "hello" in passing. Nod your head and forgive them! They may have placed a period at the end of the sentence they wrote regarding you, but God is the Author and the Finisher of your faith and your life! And get this—He loves these types of situations because they give Him the opportunity to use what appears to be the foolish things of this world (you) to confound or confuse the wise (them)! This is why I don't mind being written off. It can be annoying and hurtful sometimes, but I always find the silver lining in it, and I also find God's humor in it. "Why do the nations rage and the peoples plot in vain? The kings of the earth set themselves, and the rulers take counsel together, against the Lord and against his Anointed, saying, 'Let us burst their bonds apart and cast away their cords from us.' He who sits in the heavens laughs; the Lord holds them in derision. Then he will speak to them in his wrath, and terrify them in his fury, saying, 'As for me, I have set my King on Zion, my holy hill.'"

Who are the kings of the Earth? These are the people who have seats of authority and influence in any given season or setting. God is saying here that the tools, the devices and the wiles they use to suppress and oppress others will come to nothing! In other words, the weapons will be formed, BUT they will not and cannot prosper because no man has the power or the authority to override what God has spoken over your life. And while they may be kings or queens in the regions of thought they're in, they are subject to the King of kings!

There are many types of sentences, but they all have to end at some point. How they end is up to you. Don't get stuck in mediocrity just because people have written you off or because you've written yourself off.

The Period Between Two Sentences

Let's look briefly at another type of sentence. Google defines this sentence as: "a set of words that is complete in itself, typically containing a subject and predicate, conveying a statement, question, exclamation, or command, and consisting of a main clause and sometimes one or more subordinate clauses." Of course, this is the sentence we learned about in English class, but we'll be looking at how it applies to our regions of thoughts. Again, another word for region of thought is season. Every season is like a sentence. It has a subject (you), a verb (your choices) and a complete idea (God's will). Your life is a story that you're telling; it's a story that God wants to read to others so that He can be glorified. Your story is built up of several sentences, and every time you complete a sentence, God places a period at the end of that sentence. In the English language, a period finalizes a statement (more on this shortly), but the period that God places at the end of each season is called a transition. We'd all love to believe that we jump out of one season and into another, and while this may be true in some instances, we oftentimes need those periods so that the residue of the last season will fall off us and so that we can heal. After all, we aren't just leaving a mindset, we are sometimes losing relationships and being tossed into a completely new and foreign world. But before God places a period at the end of a sentence, that sentence has to make sense to us. For example, look at this sentence: "Make forth me matter lamp grade soup shop rock paint yes." We readily recognize the words used, but when they are paired together, they don't make sense! The same is true for us. When our choices don't match God's will for us, our seasons won't make sense to us! Consequently, we end up stuck; the musical phraseology for this is, we end up on loop! In other words, we go in circles around the same mountains on a different day. This is called a stronghold. A stronghold is a cycle; it is a fixed system within a system. Think about the clay in the container example we discussed earlier. The container has a specific capacity and a specific shape. It can only hold so much clay. Additionally, the clay in the container can only retain the shape of the container; the only exception to this rule is if the clay does not fully fill the container. If this was the case, I could make a small bunny rabbit and place it in the center of a container and it would retain its shape because it's too small to make any impact. We discussed cliques earlier. Think about that one girl who clearly doesn't fit into a clique, but somehow, has managed to get in. Maybe it's because she's related to one of the girls or she may be serving as a security guard (of sorts) for that clique. We've all seen this! They know that she's loyal and they know that she'll physically defend them, so they invited a system within their system to ensure their safety. As long as she's their friend, she would have to retain the shape of her soul; she'd have to remain confrontational, vengeful and angry. There would be no room for growth while she's within that fixed system. She'd be the equivalent of that tiny bunny rabbit. She'd be too small to make any impact within the clique, so they'd decorate her and try to make her look like themselves, but they'd ensure that she kept her mindset. If she were to start wearing makeup, heels and acting super-girly on her own, and if she became less violent and less confrontational, she'd probably be ousted from the clique. Why? Because she is a part of a whole other system. When two systems merge, they form a network, but when one system is integrated into another system, that system loses its individual identity. Think of a car and a radio. Someone integrated the two systems at some point, so now, cars have radios, but radios don't have cars. This means that you're probably not gonna get in your car often just to listen to the radio. The radio is just a feature or an amenity, but outside of the car, the radio has its own separate identity. When you approach it, you're doing so because you want to benefit from it. When one human uses another human, but both people benefit from their dealings, they form what we call a relationship or, better yet, a symbiotic relationship. The relationship can be platonic or non-platonic. When one human uses another human, but only the user benefits from their dealings, the Bible classifies the user as an enemy of the person he or she is using. This is also referred to as parasitism. Matthew 5:44 reads, "But I say unto you, Love your enemies, bless them that curse you, do good to them that hate you, and pray for them which despitefully use you, and persecute you." Why are they classified as enemies? Think of the radio. If you were the loyal fighter, and a clique of super-girly women integrated you into their clique for the sake of getting you to protect them, you will begin to lose your identity. In other words, you'll take on the shape of their souls and you'll take on the shape of what they're building. This works against your God-assigned purpose; this is what the Bible refers to as conformation. Within a fixed system, you can only serve a certain role. And while they would insist that you remain violent, loyal and confrontational, they would strategically begin to remove every other trait that they feel is working against what they want to build. This is called an enemy; in today's world, they are referred to as friendly enemies or "frenemies." So, when God read your sentence, it wouldn't make sense. It would read like, "Warrior clay mask cast brush entitlement tutorial makeup wall." God won't put a period at the end of this! No! He'd allow you to stay in that season until you opened your eyes, put back on your authenticity and do what He designed you to do! Of course, He didn't design you to be violent towards people; you may be a warrior for the Kingdom of God, but you haven't necessarily realized this yet, so you've been going after people, namely bullies. Some women noticed you before you realized who you were and invited you into their clique, but you were that radio inside of a car. You lost your identity while dealing with them. So, God will confuse the language of what they're building so that He can drive you out of it. He'll allow you to feel the pressure and the pain of Him transforming you back into the woman He designed you to be; this way, you'll never fall into the trap of conformation again. That is, until you know and accept your identity! Once you make peace with who you are, He can send you into systems to bring others out of it, but in order to invade those systems, you may have to take the shape of them. Apostle Paul said it this way, "For though I be free from all men, yet have I made myself servant unto all, that I might gain the more. And unto the Jews I became as a Jew, that I might gain the Jews; to them that are under the law, as under the law, that I might gain them that are under the law; to them that are without law, as without law, (being not without law to God, but under the law to Christ,) that I might gain them that are without law. To the weak became I as weak, that I might gain the weak: I am made all things to all men, that I might by all means save some. And this I do for the gospel's sake, that I might be partaker thereof with you" (1 Corinthians 9:19-23). Notice the why behind what he did! Apostle Paul said that he might gain the more; this is evangelism! If you go into a system because you're still in love with that system, and you try to use evangelism as a cover, you will be like the guy who kept running between the Will of God and Sin just to eat a blackberry. At some point, that window will close. That window is called a period! From there, you'll find yourself growing more and more bitter towards the church. You'll come against what you'll call "religious folks" because you're now a part of a different system and you despise anyone who doesn't dabble between the systems like you do. Don't get me wrong. There are people out there who have more religion than they do love, and they've hurt a lot of people, but you'll judge and categorize everyone who promotes holiness; you'll deem them to be religious, and you'll turn every heart that will listen to you against holiness. We've seen a huge influx of this over the last two decades, and it's only going to get worse.

Every sentence continues until it's stopped by a period. Again, this is the time of transition. It's the space in which God mends your heart and helps you to understand some of the events from the last season. He does this so you won't add a comma where He placed a period. If you add a comma to a sentence, it doesn't end; it starts another idea. It serves as a door between two seasons. Blame is adding a comma where a period should have been. The period that believers must draw is called a conclusion. At the end of every sentence, God listens intently to what we say about the people we've encountered, the experiences we've had and the wrongs we've endured. He listens for a conclusion. If we have blame on our lips, we are pretty much saying that we're still in the shape of that particular season. In other words, we didn't learn anything. This is when we find ourselves on the wrong side of that period that God has placed between us and our next season; instead, we end up on loop, recycling the same issues and regurgitating the same conversations. When we take accountability, on the other hand, we have drawn a conclusion. This is when God places us on the right side of that period; this is what legalizes our entry into the next season.

BEND IT, BIND IT, BOND IT

Matthew 18:18: Truly, I say to you, whatever you bind on earth shall be bound in heaven, and whatever you loose on earth shall be loosed in heaven.

My brother has always underestimated the power of his genius. We grew up poor, so our parents couldn't afford to buy us most of what we saw advertised on television. We had to wait until Christmas to get new toys, so we had to be innovative. We had to use whatever perishable objects around the house that we could find to make our own toys. Like most boys, my brother wanted toy guns, and not just plastic shaped objects that couldn't do anything. He wanted something that actually fired (and hurt). In the neighborhood that we were living in, you could almost always find two-by-fours. These flat pieces of wood were often discarded pieces of building material that builders had been using to repair the homes in our neighborhoods. In poor areas, building companies didn't see the need to clean up behind themselves, and the neighborhood children would often collect whatever was left behind and make toys or whatever they wanted to make from the wood. My brother decided to turn two-by-fours into guns. What he did was, he would get a piece of wood that was about two feet in length. He'd hammer a nail into one end of the wood, and on the other end, he'd secure a clothespin near the edge of the weapon using a rubber band or whatever binding agent he could find. After this, he would go into the bathroom and get a bunch of rubber bands from the hair bin. One by one, he would link those rubber bands together by looping one around the other, and pulling it through the center of the rubber band. He kept following this until he had about thirty rubber bands linked together as one. He would take one end of the rubber band strand and place it around the nail at the top of the makeshift gun. He would hammer the nail down to secure the rubber band. He would then use rocks, soda can tabs (his favorite) or whatever small objects he could find as bullets. He would pull the other end of the rubber band towards the clothespin. He'd place it around, for example, a soda can tab, open the clothes' pin and place the item, with the rubber band facing up, into the clothes' pin before closing it. And voila, he had a weapon. When he wanted to shoot at something or someone, he'd just push down on the clothes' pin to release the object. The rubber band would be stretched, so once released, the power of the rubber band would thrust the object forward. He's hurt a few people (including me) with his makeshift guns, and he's likely broken a few windows. He continued doing this until we moved into a better neighborhood where my mother absolutely forbade him from making those weapons.

I learned how powerful unity is by just looking at the rubber bands my brother used to make those guns. First and foremost, let me go on record with this—I'm not saying that he came up with the idea for that gun. It very-well could have been something he learned from someone else, but I never saw anyone else making them, and the neighborhood boys would often ask him to make a gun for them. He would often have shooting contests with some of the neighborhood boys to see whose gun would shoot the furthest. Howbeit, I remember that he preferred the small, almost rigid rubber bands. He did not like the bigger, more flexible ones because they were too thin and they had too much give. This didn't allow them to have much power behind them. He liked to link the small ones together because this would allow whatever object he was shooting out of his makeshift weapon to travel at a greater distance. Here's what I took from that:

1. Stay small (humble).
2. There is power in unity.
3. The more you're stretched, the more power there will be behind you.
4. All boundaries aren't necessarily violated physically.

My brother got in a lot of trouble because of his makeshift guns. He would fire them off into the air, and in many (if not most) of those cases, we wouldn't see how far his "bullets" would travel. We watched them fire off into the distance, not knowing how far they'd gone and where they'd land. But there had been a time or two when my parents had been visited by angry neighbors who had been "impacted" by those soda tabs or rocks. The problem was, we didn't necessarily understand boundaries. And to be honest, I think this is true for most people who live in poverty or beneath the poverty line. As a matter of fact, having escaped that world, I dare to say this—poverty is often a product of:

1. A lack of information.
2. Dishonor.
3. Rebellion.
4. Fear.
5. A blatant disregard of boundaries.

Of course, all of these pointers could be traced to the first point, and that is a lack of information.

My parents were doing the best with what they knew, but they couldn't teach us what no one had ever taken the time to teach them. Don't get me wrong—both of my parents were extremely intelligent and somewhat educated. I would even dare to say that my dad is a genius. But being intelligent doesn't necessarily equate to being informed. There are a LOT of geniuses living beneath the poverty line. They have more ideas because they have more problems that need to be solved. But again, we didn't fully understand boundaries. We understood the basics, which included staying out of our neighbors' yards unless invited over, cleaning up our own trash, respecting our elders and doing what our parents told us to do. And we weren't that great at this.

Let's look at a few definitions before we go any further. These definitions were taken from Merriam-Webster's online dictionary:

Band:

- something that confines or constricts while allowing a degree of movement
- something that binds or restrains legally, morally, or spiritually
- a strip serving to join or hold things together: such as
  - a belt
  - a cord or strip across the back of a book to which the sections are sewn

Bend:

- to constrain or strain to tension by curving
- to turn or force from straight or even to curved or angular
- to force from a proper shape
- to force back to an original straight or even condition

Bind:

- to make secure by tying; to tie together
- to confine, restrain, or restrict as if with bonds
- to put under an obligation
- to constrain with legal authority

Bond:

- something that binds or restrains
- a binding agreement
- a band or cord used to tie something
- a uniting or binding element or force
- an obligation made binding by a forfeit of money
- one who provides bail or acts as surety

What do these words have in common? It's simple. They are

all derivatives of the word "bound." Let's establish a few facts:

1. Anything that binds two or more people together is called a bond.
2. A bond that God is not a part of is called bondage.
3. A band is a tangible object (think wedding band) that serves as a visual aid representing the binding contract between two or more people.
4. The real bonding agent in a marriage is the hus*band*. God gave the husband the head position. One of his roles is to monitor the band that links him to his wife, and vice versa.
5. The threat to a bond is called a bend. Anything that can be bent, can be broken. Satan puts pressure on the bands and the bonds, hoping to break up covenant relationships and anything that the Lord has brought together.
6. While love never fails, it is not enough to secure a bond. Bonds are secured by honor, respect, trust and information. When these agents come together, they produce an unbreakable bond that hell cannot rip apart.

Marriage is the coming together of two people; we all know this. After the vows have been said and the couple has kissed, the pastor normally ends by saying, "Introducing to you for the first time, Mr. and Mrs. _____." In this, he or she is letting the onlookers know that the two are no more, but now, they are twain; they are one person, even though our eyes still see two individuals. Earth doesn't just acknowledge the couple as a unit, Heaven acknowledges them as a unit as well. On Earth, they have a binding agreement called a marriage certificate; in Heaven, they have a verbal agreement called a bond. And the moment they became one, they formed a band. Again, anything that's able to be bent can be broken. Satan then comes and immediately begins to put pressure on their bond, but he does this using their individuality. Notice that within the word "individual," you'll find the prefix "div," which is where we get "divide" and "divorce." This is also where we get "divination." The strength of a marriage or any organization is in the unit. The weakness is in the individuals. Satan looks for the weakest person in any group setting, and he begins to bend that person mentally and emotionally. But he can't just walk up to folks and start putting pressure on them. Instead, he uses the people we're connected to in order to put pressure on our covenants. Think about the rubber band gun my brother loved to create. Every rubber band was connected to another rubber band, but the rubber band attached to the nail would have to endure more pressure because it was the first band in the bunch. The second rubber band would endure the next greatest amount of pressure, and then the third; this continued until you reached the last rubber band. The last rubber band would be put under intense pressure as well, but not as much as the first rubber band. In a marriage, the husband is the first band in this network. He should be directly connected to Jesus. The wife should be connected to the Lord as well, but the husband is the head of the home.

- **Ephesians 5:22-24 (ESV):** Wives, submit to your own husbands, as to the Lord. For the husband is the head of the wife even as Christ is the head of the church, his body, and is himself its Savior. Now as the church submits to Christ, so also wives should submit in everything to their husbands.
- **1 Corinthians 11:3 (ESV):** But I want you to understand that the head of every man is Christ, the head of a wife is her husband, and the head of Christ is God.

The enemy will grab either end of that band because ultimately, the greatest amount of pressure will fall on the first in line. When my brother made his makeshift weapons, he didn't use weak rubber bands. He would fumble through the hair bin, grabbing the smallest and strongest ones. The ones that had a small tear or that appeared to be thin would remain in the bin because any amount of pressure was enough to pop them. The nail holding the first rubber band would also put pressure on it, since it had been nailed down into the wood on top of the band. Once the rubber bands lost their elasticity or when the main ones popped, he'd grab a new bunch of rubber bands. Again, the enemy will grab the couple by either end. Statistics show that more than 80 percent of divorces today are initiated by women. Why, oh why is it the woman who asks for the divorce? The answer is in the scriptures! 1 Peter 3:7 states, "Likewise, husbands, live with your wives in an understanding way, showing honor to the woman as the <u>weaker vessel</u>, since they are heirs with you of the grace of life, so that your prayers may not be hindered." The woman is the weaker vessel! But she's only partly at fault! Pay attention. Apostle Peter warned husbands to live with their wives in an UNDERSTANDING WAY! What does this mean?! After all, we say things like, "Men are from Mars and women are from Venus." Satan knows something that more than 80% of men and women don't know, and that is—where there is no understanding, there can be no grace! Another word for grace is "give." Another word for give is "elasticity." In other words, when a man does not make a concerted effort to understand his wife and to understand the female gender as a whole, he lessens the amount of tension that his marriage can endure. The same is true on the other end of the spectrum. When a wife does not make a concerted effort to understand her husband and to understand the male gender as a whole, she puts a great amount of pressure on her husband. Consequently, the couple break up and start quoting facts, not truths! They blame one another, and then, they go back into the bin and wait for someone else to pick them. By this time, they are too weak to endure any amount of pressure; this is why 60 percent of second marriages end in divorce and 70 percent of third marriages end in divorce! But what type of pressure are they dealing with? The pressures of life, of course, but the greatest amount of pressure comes when one or both parties cross an illegal boundary OR one or both individuals create and try to enforce unrealistic boundaries. Let's revisit the topic of Sin versus the Will of God, with both places being countries. One of the most common boundaries that is often crossed is called infidelity. Let's say that the blueberry on the other side of that boundary is named Mandy. Greg is a married man. His wife, Sherry, is beautiful, anointed and busy! She started a gift basket business three years ago, and it has pretty much taken over her life. Nevertheless, she still manages her house well. But because she's busy, Sherry has sacrificed something that her husband once cherished. Sherry doesn't like to spoon. She gets hot too easily, plus, she rarely comes to bed when her husband turns in. She sees spooning as foreplay, but for her husband, it's an act of intimacy. It used to strengthen his bond with her, especially when they would spoon and talk about their dreams. But nowadays, Sherry has become religious in her dealings with her husband. In other words, a lot of what she does is performance-based, including sex. She does it because it's her wifely duty, not because she loves her husband. And the truth is, she does love her husband, but she needs to get back to the basics.

One day, her husband looked over into Sin and saw Mandy. Mandy would often jog by him at the park, but at first, Greg didn't notice the petite blonde. That all changed the day that Greg went jogging, not to exercise, but to get away from Sherry. They'd had another argument about her inability to bond with her husband the proper way. While running his last mile, Greg ran into Mandy, knocking her completely off her feet. "Oh my goodness!" he shouted. "Are you okay? I'm so, so sorry! I don't know what I was thinking!" Mandy grabbed Greg's extended hand and pulled herself up. "It's okay," she said giggling. "That was the closest thing to a hug that I've gotten in a long time." The two laughed, and then, introduced themselves. As it turned out, Mandy was a divorced mother of one; she was an accountant, a cheerleading coach and a woman who loved to race cars. She was beautiful, girly and sporty—she was a man's dream girl! Greg found her attractive, but initially, he hadn't had an impure thought regarding her. This all changed three months later when he'd gone to Mandy's house for the fourth time. He'd gone there to set up her new aquarium. Mandy's daughter, Emma, had just left for school.

Once Greg was done with the aquarium, he called Mandy's name, but she didn't answer. After calling her name three times, he went down the hall towards her bedroom to investigate. That's when he saw Mandy lying on the bed. It was clear that she had been crying. "Are you okay?" he asked. "Did I do something wrong?" Mandy sat up on her bed and gestured for Greg to sit down. After a minute of silence, she finally answered. "No. It's not you. I apologize. I just got a call from Emma's dad, and he's planning to take me to court for custody of our daughter. I mean, Greg, I don't understand it at all! I married the guy and was completely faithful to him! Completely! And he cheated on me with our next-door neighbor, and do you want to know what his excuse was?! He said that I was too needy. How? Just because I insisted that he take me on a date at least once a week, plus, I loved to sit up for hours on end and talk to him.

Oh yeah, and I like to spoon! There, I said it! I'm a spooner! I'd rather sit up all night and stare into my husband's eyes than for us to be in separate rooms doing our own thing!" In that moment, Greg's heart felt something for Mandy that it shouldn't have felt. He sat down on the bed and opened his heart regarding his marriage to Sherry. "My wife's the same way," he said. "I just want to hold her sometimes, but she's always in her office putting together gift baskets. After she's done, she can't stop thinking and talking about her business, her customers and her feelings. Sometimes, I think I'm just there for moral support." After twenty more minutes of talking, Greg found himself staring into the eyes of Mandy and she reciprocated. "Can I hold you?" he asked. "I don't want anything else. Just let me hold you." Two years later, Greg divorced Sherry and married Mandy.

What happened here? Better yet, who's at fault? They both are! Satan put pressure on both ends of that band; his goal was to destroy their bond! Sherry didn't know how to multitask! There are many professional women out there who manage multi-million-dollar businesses, but they still manage to be exceptionally great wives! Greg was a terrible band or husband! He felt the pressure that the enemy had placed on his marriage and he broke! He should have sat his wife down and said, "Listen, something has to change. We have to get counseling because if we keep going at this rate, our marriage won't survive." Instead, blame caused him to cross one boundary after another until he found himself in a soul tie with a woman who was not his wife. He'd crossed into her lane at the park, but this was an accident. Every event between the two after this produced an environment for their relationship to grow and blossom. The more Greg crossed that boundary into Sin, the more pressure was put on his bond with his wife. Eventually, the rubber band broke, and when he looked at his wife, he felt nothing. Absolutely nothing! What did they need? Information; that's all! Sherry needed to learn how to be a wife and run a business at the same time. Greg needed to learn how to handle being married to a visionary. Both people needed more information so they could give each other more grace!

Greg was an individual. Sherry was an individual. But when they married, they gave up their individualism to build on their marriage. They'd already mastered being individuals, but individuals don't do well in marriages because individuals think about themselves! But somehow, when that spirit of divide came into their home, they didn't bind it. Whatever you don't bind will come after your bond! In the Old Testament days, the first year of marriage was dedicated to bonding. Deuteronomy 24:5 reads, "When a man takes a new wife, he shall not go out in the army, nor shall he be subjected to anything associated with it. He shall remain free for his home for one year and delight his wife, whom he has taken." Nowadays, we take seven-day vacations, call them honeymoons and then return back to work! In truth, couples need more time to bond, but sadly for this generation, we have to bond in our spare time, which we don't have that much of. Greg wasn't a bad guy and Sherry wasn't a bad woman. Mandy may have even been a relatively decent woman, but they were all broken. But before I go any further, let me explain what I said about them not doing their due diligence and giving up their individualism. I'm not saying that we are to lose ourselves in marriage. What I am saying is that we've mastered being individuals, but when we get married, we are still rookies in that realm. We have to strengthen our legs over there before we start demanding our "space." Space without substance is an opportunity for the enemy! Mature couples who've built solid foundations and created Godly systems know how to be individuals without compromising the strength of their marriages. Most new couples cannot do this, even though a million will shout that they are an exception to this rule; that is, until the newness wears off! After that, they start saying that they grew apart, not realizing that the "space" they gave each other served as a growing gulf in their marriage, and by the time they realized what they'd done, they couldn't reach one another. This is why we need menders or, better yet, mentors. Mentors give us the glue (information) that we need to secure our bonds.

The aforementioned story doesn't just apply to marriages, it applies to any and every covenant relationship that we make ourselves a part of! Every band or unit has a bend, and every bend can only withstand a certain amount of pressure before it breaks. I talked about this silly game my brother and I used to play called Mercy. We would bend each other's fingers back as far as we could, and when it became too painful, we would scream, "Mercy!" If I'd kept pulling his finger after he'd screamed for mercy, I could have potentially broken his finger. Every bend has the potential to destroy a bond, and if a band or a bond is broken, you can't just put the two objects back together. You would need some type of binding agent. If you used the wrong binding agent, the bond between the two items would be too weak to withstand any pressure. This is why God created boundaries. They protect the bonds that hold our relationships together.

SPIRITUAL HEART ATTACKS

"Keep thy heart with all diligence; for out of it are the issues of life" (Proverbs 4:23).

Reminders:
1. Your soul can be broken up into many states; the enemy seeks to advance through each of these states so that he can conquer each one, and eventually rule your heart.
2. Your region of thought is the season you're in. In other words, your mindset and your current season are synonymous.

There has to be something valuable in the heart, otherwise, God wouldn't have told us to guard it. But what does it mean to guard your heart? Think of a security guard at a bank. His job isn't just to stand there and be an ornamental fixture; his job is to protect the customers, the employees and the money that's stored in that particular bank. To guard your heart simply means to defend it. It means to draw boundaries around it so that crooks and liars won't be able to access it. What's interesting is, when a thief goes into a bank, in most cases, he won't go anywhere near the vault; this is where the majority of the bank's wealth is stored. The bank tellers normally don't have a lot of money in their registers, nevertheless, most thieves target the bank tellers. This is because it takes more time, effort and planning to break into a vault.

Your heart is your vault; it contains all of the issues of your life. Everything that you'll ever be is already stored within your heart. When you plug yourself into Jesus and follow Him in every state of your being, a light comes on (we call this revelation), and this is when you begin to discover, not just who you are, but you discover your superpowers. You discover your strengths and you come to understand your weaknesses. This is why Satan is so attracted to your heart, but amazingly enough, like a bank robber, Satan doesn't always go directly for the kill. Oftentimes, he attacks the people around you so that he can get to you. Sometimes, he attacks you to get to the people around you. Yes, he's strategic like that. For example, I was married and in my mid-twenties when an old friend of mine called. Before she'd called, my ex and I were running around the house playing with each other. We were tickling each other, hiding from each other and just acting silly. We were laughing it up when my phone rang. I rushed over and picked it up while my ex excused himself to go to the bathroom. That's when I heard my friend crying hysterically. "What's wrong?" I asked, already knowing the answer to my question. Her husband was at it again. "You need to leave him!" I yelled. "He's not trying to change! I don't know why you keep putting up with him!" It was as if all the joy got sucked out of my house just like that. I found myself giving her the same advice that I'd been giving her for months. "Leave!" It was clear that her husband didn't want to be married, and quite frankly, I couldn't understand why she was so adamant about making it work. After encouraging her for a few minutes, she finally said, "Thank you. I feel so much better!" With that, she let out a sigh of relief as if she'd just had the best bowel movement of her life. She thanked me again, reiterating how good she felt, and then, we hung up. But when we hung up, I was mad. No, I was livid. "Can you believe this guy?!" I shouted at the bathroom door. "She said he didn't even bother to come home last night! I don't know why she keeps putting up with him! I would have left his stupid butt a long time ago!" I kept ranting on and on until my ex stuck his head out of the bathroom and looked at me. "You're stupid," he said. "You and I were having a good time, and you just let that girl steal a precious moment from us. And she still isn't going to leave him. She'll be cuddled up with him tonight." With those words, he closed the bathroom door, and I was left speechless. But he was somewhat right. I wasn't stupid, but what I'd done was stupid. I hadn't guarded my heart. Consequently, I'd just made an uneven exchange over the phone. She'd zapped all of my energy and joy out in that moment, and in exchange, she'd given me her frustration, her anger and her anxiety. For the rest of that day, the atmosphere in my house was very uncomfortable. I often share this story with married couples anytime, for example, a husband complains about his wife's friends or vice versa. I look at the wife and say, "You do realize that if Satan wants to attack your marriage, he'll attack your friends' marriages. If he can't get to you, he'll go after someone close to you!" These are the bank tellers of your soul. This is why you have to also guard your peace. You guard your peace by guarding your heart. And to be fair, I did the same thing to her on a few occasions. I'd called her when I was upset with my ex and completely stole her joy, but she wised up before I did.

If Satan wants to attack your finances, he'll attack someone close to you—someone who isn't financially responsible. It happens all the time. A woman gets her income tax refund and plans to go on vacation with it, but before she can book her flight, the phone rings. "You have a collect call from Jackson County Jail from …." Her heart drops. It's her brother, and he's been arrested again. With little time to spare, he jumps straight to the point. "Sis, they arrested me for domestic violence! I didn't hit that girl! I just pushed her off me! Can you come and bail me out? I promise I'll pay you back when I get my tax refund!" And just like that, her vacation is canceled and her brother goes home. Both of these are minor examples of spiritual heart attacks. The enemy's main focus is your heart! This is why God told you to guard it, but this is easier said than done, given the fact that most of us have never truly been taught how to guard our hearts. Below are a few tips.

1. **Create a Constitution for your heart.** Every great nation has supreme laws that govern it. Divide this Constitution into three parts: conscious, subconscious and unconscious. The people who should be filed under conscious are the folks who are irrelevant OR problematic. Look at the chart below to get a better understanding of how to classify and manage these

relationships.

Access	Description
Conscious 30 Fold	These are the people who you should deal with only when you see them or have to deal with them in some capacity or another. They can't go anywhere near your heart because they are immature, unstable, competitive and/or toxic. Love them, but keep them away from your heart. This means that you should NEVER open up and share intimate details about your life with them. You should NEVER loan them money, and whenever they visit you (if allowed), they should be restricted to the living room or the den only! You have to treat them like friendly strangers.
Subconscious 60 Fold	This is the trust category. And of course, there are levels of trust, so be sure to be specific. Some people

can be trusted in your financial state, but they cannot be trusted romantically. So, a guy friend who wants to partner with you in business may not be such a bad idea if he's financially responsible and the two of you draw up a contract, but his romantic state may be in complete ruins. And while he makes a great friend, he makes a horrible boyfriend, and an even worse husband. But he may have a level of trust with you that most folks don't have, and for this reason, you may feel comfortable sharing certain things with him.

The people in this category are the folks you trust to go beyond the living room of your home, with the most trustworthy of them being people that you would trust with a key to your home.

List the names of the people closest to you, and take inventory of their many states. The states of a human include:

- Mental state
- Physical state
- Religious state
- Parental state
- Familial state
- Platonic state
- Romantic state
- Sexual state
- Career state
- Financial state

Remember, someone can be a religious friend, but a financial foe. It is important to take inventory of where they are in each of these states; this way, the enemy can't use them in those areas to attack your heart. After all, these people are intimate with you on one level or another; they are closest to your heart, so they can and oftentimes will

	be Satan's point of access to your heart.
Unconscious 100 Fold	Nobody but God should be here, but your spiritual leaders will come closer to this arena than anyone else.

2. **Establish boundaries around every state of your soul.** Be as detailed as possible. For example, after taking inventory of your relationships, you may realize that everybody around you is broke and financially irresponsible. So, a good law to establish is, "I'm not letting people borrow money from me anymore. When they ask for money, I'll give them a book." And you can't just create these boundaries in your head. You need to write them down somewhere; this is why you need a personal Constitution.

3. **Create a grace account for everyone in your life.** Don't put anything in this account. This is your premeditated decision to forgive them for whatever crimes they commit against you. Now, don't get me wrong; this does not mean that they get to keep their positions in your heart. Just like any system, there are processes, procedures and people who have to be promoted, just like there are processes, procedures and people who have to be demoted. If someone violates a boundary more than once, you have to reevaluate your relationship with that person and

determine if he or she is mature enough for the role you gave him or her. If not, you don't necessarily have to cut that person out of your life. Sometimes, a close friend has to be demoted to a distant friend or an associate, and there's nothing wrong with this.

4. **Communicate your new boundaries with the people closest to you.** For example, I once told a friend that I was no longer going to listen to her complain anymore. I told her that she complained too much, and it was a blatant disregard for how good God had been to her. Of course, I didn't call her and just randomly say this. Instead, she called me and started complaining. I stopped her midway through her complaint and told her my new stance. She understood and we sat on the phone and talked about the goodness of the Lord. A few days later, she called me and started complaining again. I stopped her immediately and reminded her of my new policy. Now, if you have gossipers around you, the best time to communicate your new boundaries with them is whenever you speak with them. You can say, for example, "I've decided to reformat my life. One of the issues I've had was gossiping, and I've made a commitment to God to no longer gossip. I'm asking that you not only hold me accountable, but I want us to be mindful of our conversations starting right today. This is a part of my personal rehab; this is a part of my personal journey back to wholeness." Note: Reevaluate and demote every person who does not

respect your new boundaries.

5. **Practice saying no WITHOUT watering it down with an excuse.** Sure, this will be uncomfortable at first, but trust me, you'll grow comfortable over time. For example, if Jason says to you, "Hey, can I borrow thirty dollars?" Don't say, "No, because I have to pay Tommy's daycare tomorrow." Just say no or you can say, "I love you, but no." If he asks why, be honest with him. "I'm not loaning out money anymore. This is a personal decision I made to keep the peace in my relationships." Don't go any further than that. Giving too much information or making excuses only opens up a dialogue between you and Jason, where he'll attempt to challenge every one of your points. Will he be angry with you? Yeah, more than likely, but if he loves and honors you, he'll get over it. If he stops speaking to you, he's just proved that he was too close to you in the first place. The word "no" shifts the people in your life, forcing them to get into the seats that they are mature enough to sit in. Constantly saying yes to people keeps them in roles and positions that they should not have in your heart and in your life, but the word "no" (especially when used several times) will always reveal the character of each person in your life.

6. **Count the cost!** Establishing, promoting and enforcing boundaries is expensive because it will cost you some relationships! Seriously! It may even cost you some relationships that you feel you can't live

without, but this is a lie! Self-confidence comes from self-awareness. Self-confidence is built on self-esteem. And your self-esteem is one of the treasures in that little vault called your heart. If Satan can steal it, he can get you to lower your standards, discount yourself and accept whatever he tosses at you. Be aware of the fact that some people just may walk out of your life or shift you from being a dear or close friend to just someone they merely socialize with. Don't take this personally! Just heal and understand that you simply brought them too close and vice versa. If you're unaware of the cost, chances are, you won't fully follow through with these steps because the moment someone reacts negatively to your newfound boundaries, you'll return to the pit that God is trying to dig you out of. Bound people hate boundaries; that's a given, so they are going to respond negatively.

7. **Enforce those boundaries religiously!** Every time I talk about enforcing boundaries, I think about my company. This is because I've learned some of the greatest lessons in life through entrepreneurship. I've learned a lot of what I call "expensive lessons," and I still make them from time-to-time. It's just a part of being an entrepreneur. But what makes a successful entrepreneur is when you learn from those mistakes and you take the necessary precautions to ensure that you don't repeat them. The same is true in life. For example, I don't take "bids" to do work for people;

I don't allow them to talk me down on my prices. I don't entertain conversations about discounts. This means that I know the value of what I'm offering! I point my potential clients to one of my many sites where they can see my prices. If someone asks for a discount, I tell them that no discounts are available. I don't go into a long-winded discussion about me having bills to pay. I just say no. Nevertheless, maybe once a year for the first seven years in business, I've made the mistake of letting someone talk me into giving them a better offer, and this has backfired one hundred percent of the time! Once you remove one boundary, you may as well remove them all because they are not going to respect any boundary that you try to enforce! They'll see all of your boundaries as negotiable. If you say that no one can smoke in your house, don't lift these boundaries just because your uncle who you haven't seen for 12 years is visiting you and you don't want to offend him. BOUNDARIES ARE DESIGNED TO OFFEND THE FOLKS WHO HATE THEM! Boundaries protect systems! Your house, your peace and your sanity are all independent systems that are interdependent on one another.

What is a spiritual heart attack? First, remember that you are in a particular season. Your season is your region of thought; it's your overall mindset. It is a culmination of every state that you're in. This represents your movement or lack thereof.

Satan advances through every state that he can enter into, but his overall goal is to get to your heart. If he can pervert or attack the heart, he can stop your movement in the world and your advancement in the Kingdom. So, if he enters through your familial state, this simply means that he's using your family (or lack thereof) to attack your identity, your self-worth, your self-esteem and your self-perception. He will stop at nothing to advance from this state into other states, but the problem is, you keep moving! You keep praying! You keep forgiving! You keep planning for your future! In other words, you have not given up; you have not fainted! You keep advancing from one region of thought to another, and this makes it difficult for him to keep up with you. So, he has to find a way to stall you. He has to find a way to get you comfortable so that you either won't move, or if you do move, you'll struggle with procrastination, meaning, you will be sluggish in your movements. My pastor, Apostle Bryan Meadows, always says, "Your blessing travels at the speed of your obedience." In other words, if you are slow to obey God, you will cause your own blessings and breakthroughs to be delayed. Again, Satan will stop at nothing to stall you; this way, he can advance in every area of your life. He knows that while a season isn't a time-stamped event, God often does put a timer on each season! That's what grace is! It's the space and the time for you to wake up, sober up and move on! This is why we coined the term "grace period."

Within every region of thought, you'll find what I like to refer to as boxes; these are the comfort zones that we burrow in.

The problem with the human soul is that it can adapt to just about any and every condition! If you throw a man into a tiny four-by-four jail cell, he'll adapt. If a man has to sleep under a bridge every day, he'll adapt. If you toss a woman into an abusive relationship, over time, she'll adapt. The human soul is amazing because it is resilient! Again, when we adapt to certain regions of thought, we become masters of that region of thought. Another word for a person who has mastered a region of thought is a manipulator. In other words, he or she has learned to work the system of that particular season. When we enter into new seasons, we come into those seasons as babes or unlearned people! We're oftentimes weary from the transition and we're still trying to adjust to some of the many changes that we've endured during the transition, for example, we often lose friends while in transition. As a result of this, we sometimes enter into new seasons alone or the only friends we have left are often distant friends. By distant, I mean:

1. We don't talk to them often.
2. We don't talk to them often BECAUSE they are several seasons behind us or several seasons ahead of us.
3. We don't share intimate details about our lives with them, and vice versa.

So, when manipulators or people who've mastered the seasons that we're entering approach us, they often look like blessings. We're excited to meet them because they come off as friendly, knowledgeable, confident, helpful and down-to-earth. When you've just entered a new season, you enter that season as a babe or a rookie. In other words, you are unlearned! You don't know where to go, what to do, who to hang around and who to avoid. When you come across people who've mastered that particular season, they will look like heroes to you in the beginning. This is because, just like any organization, when you initially enter into a new region of thought, you will come across a lot of cliques. And because you still look and smell like your last season, many of them won't be open to getting to know you. Instead, most of your attempts to make friends may be futile. But all of a sudden, someone will approach you and offer to help you whenever you appear to be lost. That person may be nice and that person may be helpful, but he or she may have also mastered that season. And the issue is, people like this can and do sometimes make great friends; that is, until you attempt to leave the region of thought that they've mastered. Satan's goal is to use these people to create (illegal) soul ties with you. By illegal I mean that you didn't test the spirit, and because of this, you gave that person a seat in your heart or role in your life that he or she was not mature enough to have. You were supposed to guard your heart. In other words, you didn't resist the temptation to tell that person everything there is to know about you, and just like a romantic relationship, you should have taken your time, guarded your heart and tested the spirit behind these people. But you didn't, and they moved right into your heart. From there, they:

1. Boxed you into their opinions of you.

2. Introduced you to "their" cliques.
3. Assigned you a role in that clique!
4. Gave you a nickname OR emphasized one of your characteristics, while ignoring the rest. For example, you may be a serious, level-headed person who is ambitious and goal-oriented. But you have a unique sense of humor, even though this isn't your strong suit. Your new friend decides that she wants a clown for her clique, so every time you say something funny or something that is remotely funny, she laughs hysterically and says, "This is why I love being around you! You are crazy!" She introduces you to people as her silly friend by saying things like, "This is the girl I was telling you about! She will have you laughing until you pass out, and half of the time, she doesn't even realize that she's said something funny! She'll try to breeze right past it ..." From that moment on, all you can be is silly. People will always feed in you what they want to see grow, all the while starving those strengths, characteristics or weaknesses that they feel aren't benefiting them.

This is a spiritual heart attack, and every person who has graduated from more than one region of thought can supply you with the names of the folks who "adopted" and categorized them when they'd entered into new seasons. And these were the very-same people that they had to pray out of their lives when God started to promote them; these were the people who the prophets were talking about when they prophesied, "God's about to remove some people from your life." And when God promotes a person, it doesn't always look like man's idea or concept of a promotion. Kingdom promotion looks like God:

1. Increasing your capacity to retain information. In other words, you won't fall asleep while reading the Bible or any other book, and God will open your eyes to understand what you're reading.
2. Giving you access to books, seminars and events; in other words, God will set a table for you to get and eat the information.
3. Giving you mentors after His own heart. In other words, God will strengthen your spiritual digestive system; this way, you can digest or understand the information. This is what allows you to retain it.
4. Opening doors for you to practice and apply what you just learned.

When you come across new people, the Bible tells you to test the spirit; this means that your job isn't to be super friendly and fear hurting their feelings. This is where most people mess up! Your job is to be kind and patient, but guarded! This doesn't look like you accepting an invitation to every event they invite you to; this doesn't look like you sitting on the phone with them for hours on end, talking about your childhood, your children, your dreams, your nightmares and your fears. No, if they are good and Godly people, they will also be patient! Anyone who is in a rush to create and strengthen a soul tie with you is a problem in the making! And when you befriend a mastermind without testing that spirit, he or she will introduce you to your new season using his or her own perception and lingo as a guide. For example, let's say that you're a woman who's just started going to a new college. You don't know anyone there yet, but you are eager to make friends. (This is why the Bible tells us to be anxious for nothing!) You see a group of girls that you think you can relate to. You sit near their table in the cafeteria everyday, but they don't invite you over. You've complimented a few of them, let one of the ladies copy your paper during a test and you've even defended one of the girls when another girl was trying to fight her. By all intents and purposes, they should invite you, at minimum, to sit with them, but they don't. Why? You don't fit. That's the simple answer. The complicated answer is—they recognize leadership in you, and they already have a leader. Anything that has two heads is a freak!

One day, another woman from an entirely different clique approaches you. Please note that, in most cases, the members of a clique won't invite you into their circle. They can't do this because they're members. Most of the time when you're invited into a circle, it's by the leader of that clique. Members will tell their clique's leaders about you, hoping that he or she will invite you to an event, but for the most part, a member can never and will never invite you to come and sit with her and her friends. A member can be friendly towards you in your third period class because none of her friends are in that class, but if you take fourth period with her, she may completely ignore you or she may appear to be relatively distant. She may be friendly and she may speak to you, but that will be the furthest she'll go. Nevertheless, the leader from an entirely different clique approaches you after noticing you and some guy who's been staring at you having a moment. He looks at you and smiles, and you return the favor. Suddenly, a voice whispers in your ear, "If I were you, I'd avoid him. He's slept with two-thirds of the freshmen population at this school, and word on the street is, he's giving away more than sex, if you catch my drift." You look over and see a beautiful, spunky and fashionable young lady. Your laugh almost interrupts her introduction. "Oh, I'm sorry. Where are my manners? My name is Raven, but my friends call me Rai. You can call me Rai." You've seen Raven around the campus, and she almost always appears to be having fun with her friends. "I'm Yvette," you say. "And thank you for warning me. That guy stares at me everyday. I just smile back at him so things don't get weird." Raven laughs and compliments your new hair color. "That's cute. Is that auburn?" The two of you talk, and in the next class, Raven invites you to sit with her and her friends. Before long, she starts filling you in about the people you take classes with, the teachers and anyone else you encounter. What is she doing? She's telling you how she sees the people; she's orientating you into her clique! If you are going to be a part of her clique, you will have to adopt her perception! In short, she's telling you how to think. For every person that she attaches a negative label to, you won't be able to socialize with that person without there being some type of repercussion! She's initiating you into her highlights your sense of humor, you have no choice but to be the clown of that clique. I urge you to be friendly, but don't take the bait! Take your time with her, and if she highlights your funny side, be sure to show her your serious side more than you show her your funny side. Don't be manipulated into becoming a sideshow.

But let's say that you allow her to mold you until you finally fit in. One day, you decide to change your major. You no longer want to be a licensed Mental Health Counselor, you decide that you want to get your Doctoral Degree in Psychology. This change means that you won't be taking some of the classes that you've been taking with Raven. It also means that you'll have a higher degree than Raven, and she's not about to be shown up! You tell your clique-leader about your plans, but she doesn't seem to be too thrilled. She's worked way too hard and invested far too much to see it all go to waste in you. So, she tries to talk you out of it, claiming that the classes are difficult, if not impossible. She urges you to continue the route you've been on, and she says that after you get your Master's Degree, you should then weigh out all of your options. But your mind is made up. You've prayed about it and you have peace with your decision, so you lovingly reject Raven's offer; instead, you excitedly tell her about your plans. The next day, you discover that neither she nor any of the women in her clique are speaking to you. This is because you do not and cannot fit into the role she has assigned you to, and that's okay! Every innovator has had a Raven in his or her life! Some of us have tolerated them for decades on end! Sadly enough, we've also seen men and women with earth-shattering potential who've thrown away their authenticity just to satisfy the Raven in their lives, and they became masters of the seasons that they got stuck in! I wanted to share this example of a spiritual heart attack so that you won't think that it's always romantic! Satan will come at you through any state that he finds a way to access. Your goal is to not allow yourself to be boxed into people's opinions of who you should be and how you should be. In other words, guard your heart. The enemy passionately wants to attack it. Why? Because you're like clay. If he can shape you into what he says that you should be, and then, cause you to harden your heart while you're in that shape, he can dismantle your potential. He can place you in a box and park you in a season like a run-down car. After this, you won't pose a threat to his kingdom anymore.

And lastly, another spiritual heart attack occurs when the people you've allowed into your heart begin to attack your character, your trust and your identity. Most of the time, these people will be the ones who are closest to you, like family members and close friends. Don't take it personally. Everyone in your life will tell you the role that he or she is fitted for if you'll only listen and pay attention. For example, I don't allow gossipers anywhere near my heart. If they're in my family, I'm friendly with them, but I don't engage in gossip with them, I don't allow them to share gossip with me, and I make sure that our conversations are non-toxic. By doing this, I have essentially evicted them from my life! I never had to argue with them. I didn't have to accuse them of anything; I simply drew a set of boundaries around my ears, my eyes and my lips, and I enforced those boundaries. So, if a relative of mine calls and says, "Girl, did you hear about Jane? You know they said that her boyfriend left her for her best friend!" I'm not going to entertain that conversation. I can dismantle it by saying, "That's horrible. She's a beautiful jewel in the making, and I pray that God heals her. Do you mind if we pray for her right quick?" What did I just do? I James 4:7'ed the gossiper! Yes, you read it right! I use the scriptures as verbs when I learn to put them into action! James 4:7 states, "Submit yourselves therefore to God. Resist the devil, and he will flee from you." By speaking positively of Jane, I have caused the gossiper to feel a tinge of guilt and a whole lot of shame! She won't call me anymore; she may call me when she needs prayer, but other than that, I likely won't hear from her anytime soon. This is tested and tried. And let me say this—sometimes, people aren't gossiping when they tell you about something someone is going through, especially family members. Sometimes, they are just informing you. The way to tell the difference is by simply listening to the person. Gossipers usually take pleasure in another person's pain. Someone who's just informing you will sound concerned, and say, for example, "So, make sure you call and check on Jane." They may even request that you not tell the other person that they informed you about her situation, and this is okay. To tell the difference between an informer and a gossiper, you simply need patience and wisdom. If I can't initially tell the difference, I may say, "Oh wow. I didn't know that." If the person on the other end is a gossiper, he or she will show no concern, but will instead appear to be entertained by the drama. This is when I'll speak positively of the person the gossiper is speaking negatively of, and I'll ask if we can pray for her or him.

When you draw boundaries around your heart and you consistently, confidently and religiously enforce those boundaries, the people in the waiting room of your heart will take their proper places; they will either leave your life, take a higher seat in your life or take a lesser role than the ones they were initially applying for. This is the power and the purpose of boundaries. Boundaries put everyone and everything in place. Remember, boundaries were designed to protect the systems that God has created; this keeps them from overlapping and interfering with one another. Boundaries are also put in place to protect man-made systems as well. When you give God His proper seat in your heart, and you guard your heart with all diligence, you will learn and experience what it's like to truly love yourself. This is when you'll make peace with being alone (whenever and if ever you find yourself in a season where you're transitioning between relationships), and this is when you'll refuse to settle for the roles and the boxes that people try to stuff you into.

Boundaries and Breakthroughs

On May 18th, 2020, I received the following message on Facebook:

> "Hello Tiffany! Pray all is well! I just wanted to share a dream about you that I had recently. You were either an eagle or flying like an eagle, but you were referenced like an eagle. You had a business doing weddings and banquets for others, where people came to you. You had all these fine linens where you were very capable of doing the job."

Of course, I asked her for permission to share the dream and she gave it to me.

I immediately reflected on the dream I'd had of the woman doing my hair and makeup; this is the dream I shared of me wearing a wedding gown. In that dream, God was using someone to get me ready. In her dream, God was using me to get others ready. Of course, the eagle represents vision. In order for me to help God's people, I must be a visionary. I have to see what God sees in them, otherwise, I'd be distracted by their flesh. Visionaries are futuristic; God enables us to see in others what they can't see in themselves, both the good and the bad. Sometimes, people rush towards us because they want us to see the good in them; they want us to acknowledge their potential, but they run away from us when we see what's holding them back from reaching that potential. The Bible calls this itching ears. An amazing and interesting fact about itching is that to stop it, you have to interrupt it with pain. Sure, we apply the amount of pain to an itch that we can handle, but the point is, an itch is silenced by pain. Visionaries don't necessarily scratch ears, we open them. When we are untrained, we cut them off. And being a visionary doesn't mean that we're prophets; most of us aren't. We are simply prophetic, but not necessarily prophets. But that's not all I took from that dream. What I considered is this—eagles have an incredible amount of range. Range, in the human sense, would look like capacity.

- Eagles can fly up to 10,000 feet in the air.
- Migrating eagles can fly over two hundred miles in a single day!
- Eagles can dive! They are relatively decent swimmers who can dive up to 100 miles per hour.

This is what it looks like when God enlarges your territory. He pushes back the cuticles of your potential so that you can go higher, go deeper and go further than you've ever gone before. Like many believers, I had once been that woman who was falling down a bottomless pit, thrust into endless cycles of defeat mentally, spirituality and generationally. There was no hope for me. When the world looked at me, they saw a lost cause, even after I got saved. When I got saved, I saw that same look in the eyes of believers. They reminded me of a doctor who had just entered a hospital room to deliver the bad news to one of his patients. "I'm sorry. There's nothing else we can do." All hope appeared to be gone. That's when God delivered me with a single scripture. 1 Corinthians 1:26-29 (ESV) was my saving grace.

It reads, "For consider your calling, brothers: not many of you were wise according to worldly standards, not many were powerful, not many were of noble birth. But God chose what is foolish in the world to shame the wise; God chose what is weak in the world to shame the strong; God chose what is low and despised in the world, even things that are not, to bring to nothing things that are, so that no human being might boast in the presence of God." I wasn't designed to fit, and I eventually learned to be okay with this. Again, when I had a clique of friends, they accused me of bringing in strays, meaning, I wasn't following protocol. Cliques represent limitations, and I passionately HATE being typecast, stereotyped or placed in a box. Nevertheless, I allow people's perceptions of me to help me to understand the height of their perspective. **Bonus: And because I never fit in, I have never limited myself to a region of thought.** This means I've never stopped learning, growing or maturing! In other words, I haven't climaxed!

I had once been that woman falling down an endless pit, and my dreams would often reflect that. Like most people, I've had countless dreams of me falling, but I've never hit rock bottom. Instead, I would bounce on my bed and wake up. Because this was a common dream, I've never put that much thought into it. But nowadays, I understand that my dreams of falling had everything to do with the generational curses that I was once a casualty of. I had been born into that fall. I was raised in the middle of that fall. I dated while falling. I got saved in the middle of that fall. I got married (twice) while falling. I started buying my first home while free-falling. I got divorced (twice) while in that fall. I served God while falling. But one day, the Lord said, "Enough!" And this time, I didn't bounce up on a bed. Instead, I woke up. I sobered up. I gave up, and then, I gave in. That's when He taught me to soar. I finally surrendered to His will for my life. Now, I'd be lying if I said I've never looked back. I did look back for the first few years of my walk. There were times during my journey that I've looked back; this is because after running out of the world, I found myself running into believers who admired the pit that I'd crawled out of. They were mesmerized by the blackberries and the raspberries in Sin; they were being seduced by the big strawberries on the other side of God's will. What was I to do? Was I supposed to fit in like a zombie, turn around, start chanting Christian gibberish and proceed to walk towards what God had delivered me from? Or was I supposed to go against the grain and keep running towards Christ, knowing that by doing so, I may never find my place with people? Now, don't mistake what I'm saying. Some believers run towards the world to evangelize; this is what God called them to do. I'm not speaking about them. I'm talking about the ones who are in love with the raspberries, the blueberries, the blackberries, the strawberries and the grapes. I remember saying to God, "Lord, I don't fit! I thought things would be different when I got saved!" After all, I'm not willing to go back, even if that means I have to wear the dart that most Christians throw at the folks who go against the grain—it's the dart that has a big white banner on it, and on that banner, the word

"RELIGIOUS" is written in capital red letters. But I've learned to use that banner as my purity cloth. I've lied on it, cried on it and bled on it, and when I was done, I handed it to the Father. I decided to let Him deal with the noise while I continued to run towards what many seem to be running away from. And when He healed me, He gave me the strength, the wisdom and the zeal to run back after the very thing that had once chased and crushed me. He allowed me to go back into the darkness to snatch people out. Why? Because the minute you defeat a region of thought, you can freely cross those boundaries and not get bound; that is, unless you're crossing them for the wrong reason.

Narcissists and the Big U

Let's have another grown-up conversation. **Sex.** This is a taboo subject for many Christians, but our unwillingness to talk about it causes us to be willfully ignorant. We all know what happens at the height of a sexual encounter. One word—orgasm. Nowadays, we often reference this as the "big O" or the "big oh." First, there's stimulation, and next, there's arousal. After arousal, there's penetration, and after penetration, the encounter takes place (I'll spare you the details). Not long after that, one or both parties will experience the "big O." What's interesting about this is, if you really think about it, entering and exiting a season is very similar to sex.

- **First, there's stimulation.** This has everything to do with what we see, hear, feel, touch or crave. Something or someone inspires us to want to change our minds or, better yet, enter a new region of thought. Maybe, it was our pastors. Maybe, it was a book or a series of books. Maybe, it was a mentor, a friend or a stranger in passing. Then again, maybe, it was an enemy. I often tell people that I was inspired to chase and embrace forgiveness by simply being around bitter people. I vowed to never become like them. Either way, something inspired us to want more.
- **Next, there's arousal.** Most people don't get past being stimulated. They talk about writing the books,

starting the businesses or even drawing boundaries in their lives, but when the time comes to implement these things, they flop. This is why the Bible says a builder counts the costs before he or she builds anything. Every change has a price-tag associated with it, and if we're not willing to pay the price for change, we may as well do like the rest of the world and distract ourselves until Jesus comes back. Arousal takes place when we actually put our hands to the plow (as weird as that sounds in this context). This is when we start advancing forward and allowing ourselves to experience change.

- **After arousal, there's penetration.** This is when we escape one mindset and enter another one. In other words, we allow ourselves to, at minimum, experience a new season before deciding if we want to advance forward or withdraw back to the season we've just come out of.

- **Next, there's the actual rhythmic experience of intercourse.** When entering a new season, we are rookies. And it is for this reason that the winds of that season keep pushing us towards what we just came out of. This is why we find ourselves saying, "It seems like when I take two steps forward, I get pushed three steps back." This is the rhythm of change. When entering a new season, no one is responsible for ensuring that we remain aroused; we do this by reading books, getting mentors, showing up at church, serving at church and doing more in that season than we've done in seasons-past. While in this rhythm, we have to not only make sure that we stay excited about the season that we're in, we also have to ensure that we don't climax prematurely. In every region of thought, you will see eagles sitting on ducks' nests just because somebody finally accepted them. What happened was, they climaxed prematurely. They peaked at the bottom. For example, a woman gets the attention of a man who has a 3B curl pattern, instead of the 4C curl pattern she's used to, so she marries the guy and settles down. Yes, people marry for even more shallow reasons than this! A man gets the attention of a former prom queen who's finally lowered her standards enough for him to get her attention, so he settles down with her and climaxes in the wrong season. You have to resist the temptation to settle down in the wrong season!

- **And finally, the orgasm begins!** This is what we've been waiting for! This is the height of a new season; this is a culmination of everything we've been through while in that region of thought. We want it to be memorable and we want it to be explosive, but here's the kicker—not all orgasms are created equally. For most people, they are pleasurable, but for some, orgasms can be painful. For some, it's a combination of both pleasure and pain. When we're at the height of an old season, about to enter a period of transition where we'll be transitioning from one region of thought to another, we often feel a wide array of emotions.

First, there's the excitement that everything we've been through has finally come to a head (no pun intended). But to counter this excitement is watching the people around us take their rightful seats, and those rightful seats for some are on the outskirts of our lives. This is when we experience the most betrayal, the most rejection and the most trauma. This is why there has to be a hallway or a wilderness between the old season and the new one; we need time to process what we've just come out of. We need time to heal, to go through deliverance and to get some of our many questions answered. And this is when we typically experience what I call the "big u."

What is the "big u"? One word—ultimatum. Let's deal with narcissists, for example. These people are masters at creating soul ties with others. They meet people and immediately employ a method that psychologists refer to as "love bombing." Psychology Today defines it this way, "Love bombing is the practice of overwhelming someone with signs of adoration and attraction — think flattering comments, tokens of affection, or love notes on the mirror, kitchen table, or windshield, and you're beginning to get the picture. It's flowers delivered at work with hearts dotting the i's in your name. It's texts that increase in frequency as they increase in romantic fervor. It's surprise appearances designed to manipulate you into spending more time with the bomber — and, not coincidentally, less time with others, or on your own" (Source: Psychology Today/Love Bombing: A Narcissist's

Secret Weapon/Suzanne Degges-White Ph.D.)

In short, love-bombing is the narcissist's way of quickly entangling you in a soul tie. The typical narcissist is what we refer to in the church as the Jezebel spirit. Someone with this spirit has to entangle you in a web of deceit; this web is made up of the many soul ties they are a part of. They'll say things like, "Everyone who loves me leaves me." This is their way of unloading the guilt and the responsibility of what they've been through on you. These people go out of their way to make themselves invaluable in your life. They'll fight your enemies, help you with a bill or two and do whatever they can to get you to make them into your idol. They want to be worshiped; they have to be worshiped if they are going to stick around. But if you're studying and showing yourself approved, and if you're prayerful, God will eventually begin the process of removing these people from your life. He doesn't pull you apart from them the way Danny Glover peeled Celie off of Nettie in The Color Purple. No, God simply changes your mind. He gives you more information and more opportunities to get information. And this is when the "big U" will enter the picture. Realizing that their positions are being threatened, someone who is narcissistic or someone who's mastered a season will oftentimes start the process of re-entangling you. What does this process look like? In my experience, they begin to tighten their webs of deceit by:

1. **Trying to intimidate you.** They'll sometimes do this by raising their voices and being overly emotional.

They may even get some people you know involved so that those people can and will side with them.

2. **Threatening you.** When intimidation doesn't work, many narcissists will turn to outright threats. These threats include threats of bodily harm, threatening to keep you away from your children, threatening to divorce you (either passively or directly), threatening to expose a secret of yours, threatening to ruin your career and the list goes on.

3. **Putting you on punishment.** This is when they will temporarily remove themselves from your life to teach you a lesson. In some cases, they won't remove themselves; they'll simply stop calling you as much, or they'll try to make you jealous. For example, a friend of yours is angry with you because you are considering moving to another state. She tries to talk you out of it, but your mind is made up. She's yelled at you, gotten emotional, and she's even threatened you (passively) by saying, "I don't know if our friendship could survive if you were that far away from me." None of these tactics works, so she starts using another thread in that web; she uses your mutual friends. One day, you go to social media and see that all of your friends have been hanging out, but no one invited you. Guess what? You're officially on punishment!

4. **Financial entanglement.** This tactic usually involves the narcissist offering to, for example, finance a car for you, lease a house with you, start a business with

you, rent something with you or loan money to you. The goal is to get you under a contract with the narcissist so you can't walk away so easily. Instead, you'd find yourself entangled in their web for another three to five years. This would give the toxic soul the time he or she needs to further ensnare you.

5. **The big ultimatum.** This is when a narcissist is more direct. None of their hints or tactics have been successful, so the narcissist has one more card up his or her sleeve. If it's someone you're married to, he may walk up to you and say, "Hey, can we talk? I've been thinking about 'us' lately, and I've come to realize that it's just not working. I've tried everything to save this marriage, but I have nothing left to give to this marriage. I'll pack my things and leave tonight. By the way, I don't want anything. You can have everything."

I can't tell you how many times I've stood face-to-face with an ultimatum, realizing that if I advanced forward, I was going to lose someone dear to me, but if I stayed behind, I was going to lose myself. But what I once thought was stubbornness was really zeal coupled with passion and vision. I've looked my former seasons (friends, family members, exes and all) in the eyes, and they knew before I opened my mouth what my choice was going to be. This is because at the end of a season, I've always noticed that small window closing in the distance, and I wasn't going to let it close with me locked on the wrong side of it. Sure, I'd entered Sin to get what I wanted, but there was NOTHING and NO ONE there that I wanted more than I wanted God. This is when and where my passion ignites! At the edge of a breakthrough, I've thrown myself off of some romantic, platonic, familial and financial cliffs, thus, killing what I'd once made an idol of. At the edge or end of every season, there has to be a sacrifice. Don't you EVER allow the very thing that's supposed to be sacrificed to threaten to kill itself! Either way, it has to die!

The ultimatum is the height or the orgasmic experience of every season; that is, until you surround yourself with the right people. At the conclusion of most seasons, you may feel the pressure, the frustration, the fear, the anxiety and the upset associated with the change you see on the horizon. It can truly be a horrifying experience if you don't have leaders and/or mentors around you to articulate to you what you're going through, what you will experience and why you're going through it. And then, there's the wilderness. This season feels like pure punishment because many of the people who once meant the world to you have excused themselves from your life or they have taken a more distant role in your life. This is the after-orgasm experience; this is the wilderness season. During this phase, you will feel weary; during this season, you may even feel suicidal. Trust me, I've been there before. This is the space where you feel unloved, unwanted, misunderstood, mismanaged and forgotten. This is the space where you need to bring your leaders and mentors closer, but in most cases, you won't feel like bringing anyone close. You've been wounded by the season you've left and prejudged by the season you're approaching. And to make matters worse, you'll still hear the hurtful, and yet, annoying echoes from your former season. Nevertheless, the space between each season is your time to heal, to forgive and to get the understanding you'll need to advance forward. Otherwise, if you approach your new season while still looking like your former season, your new season will reject you. Better yet, you'll reject it. This is also the time to solidify your position. It was during this space and this grace that I learned to do like David and encourage myself in the Lord. I became bolder and more confident. More importantly, I learned to rely wholeheartedly on God. You see, when you don't have to rely on people, you take away their ability to manipulate and control you. This is why it's silly to be broke and okay with it! As you grow and mature, you will come across people with similar testimonies, and get this, you will love them with an intensity that's immeasurable and inexplicable, and they will do the same for you! This is because fake friends teach you how valuable and rare real friends are. I absolutely love and adore my friends today, and it's with a love that I can't understand or explain! It's pure because I've been purified in the fire!

Pass the test! At the end of every school year, there are a series of tests that will determine whether you will be retained or promoted. The same is true for seasons. A season can become so small that it essentially becomes a rubber band or cord wrapped around the neck of your purpose. This is why you shouldn't procrastinate to do anything that God told you to do, including getting a therapist if needed! Pass the test! If someone puts you on punishment, and then proceeds to give you an ultimatum, whether that ultimatum is direct or implied, let that person transition into another role! People will tell you who they are if you're willing to listen, not just with your ears but with your heart. And again, forgive them, take responsibility for most of what happened to the adult-sized you and keep on going! And remember, entering a new season is similar to sex! While you're in the wilderness (in the space between two seasons), you may feel weary and discouraged, but if you remain accountable with your feelings, get the healing/help you need and you find other things to stimulate you, you'll be ready to enter the next season when the time or opportunity comes. Keep in mind that you will be tempted to climax prematurely in every new season that you enter; this is because it's new. You'll be tempted to marry into a clique in every season that you enter; this is because you're a rookie and they are the experts in that region of thought. Howbeit, if you keep on progressing forward, God will use you to not just pull yourself out of the many pits life has tossed you in, but He'll use you to pull others out as well.

Growing Pains

We don't go out of a season, we grow out of a season. When we think that seasons are just time-stamped events, we often become impatient and impotent in regards to our progression. This is when we make the mistake of waiting, instead of growing. One of the boundaries that we don't often hear about is the boundary of time, after all, there are illegal boundaries that we cross; then again, there are legal boundaries that we often refuse to cross. For example, God may impress upon our hearts to leave our cities behind and start over in a city far away from what we know. This is because of familiarity. The people who live in our cities know us by the flesh, and we know them. Because of this, they've assigned a label to us, and they've placed a period at the end of that label. When this happens, believe it or not, we have constructively been placed in bondage. This type of bondage is called a reputation. Please understand that not all reputations are rightfully earned. Sometimes, they were created because of rumors, and other times, they were created because of ignorance or fear. Whenever a person, a family or a community places a period behind a label that has been assigned to you, God then has to remove you from that equation because in it, there is no room for you to grow. So, God may impress it upon your heart to leave that city behind and to put space between your heart and the hearts of the people from that place. But if you are comfortable in your constructive bondage or if you keep procrastinating, it is possible that the window that separates you from your next season will close. And this would mean that your bondage was not the result of you crossing a boundary, your bondage was the direct result of you taking God's grace for granted. Please understand that God owns this Earth and everything in it. This means that while boundaries may appear to be fixed lines for us, God can and does move them. The boundaries He places around us are what we often refer to as "hedges of protection." The point I'm making here is that boundaries can and oftentimes do move! Consider the story of Harriet Tubman. She had a window of opportunity to get away from her slave masters, so she took it. To return to the South required her to be sensitive, knowledgeable and fearless. This doesn't mean that she wasn't scared; it simply means that she didn't allow fear to talk her out of her destiny. Imagine what would have happened if she'd procrastinated; imagine what would have happened if she'd stayed behind trying to talk bound folks into following her who'd made up their minds to stay behind! That window would have closed; those boundaries would have moved, and God would have likely had to raise up another person to set the captives free. She had to move when those boundaries moved if she wanted to not just get free, but to remain free.

Again, we don't just go through a season, we outgrow seasons. This is why it is not wise to date or court when you are immature. Because the man or woman you choose for yourself today isn't necessarily the person you'd choose for yourself tomorrow had you waited until you matured. And by maturity, I'm not talking about your age, I'm talking about your non-toxic relationship with Jesus Christ, coupled with your knowledge, understanding and love of Him. (Yes, people do have toxic relationships with their perception of the Lord! They think He's punishing them, ignoring them, mishandling them or that He dislikes them, and consequently, they are always trying to beg for His forgiveness, perform for His love or prove their love for Him. Cain had a toxic relationship with the Lord, but again, this was because of his perception.) One common story is—a woman meets a man while she is still a babe in Christ. Like most women who are in that stage of development, she was anxious to be married and start a family. This is because when we're babes, we're full of voids; most of those voids are hollow spots in our souls where we lack information, and some of those voids have been created by trauma. When we're full of voids, we tend to look for people and information to serve as void-fillers. So, she met a man who said that he believed in God, but he was not into the "church thing." Nevertheless, she continued dating this guy because she could see his potential. The couple stayed together for two years, crossed a few boundaries (this is what immature people do), and eventually, exchanged vows.

But something happened that she hadn't planned for. She kept growing and she kept maturing, but her new husband had no desire to change. He loved the skin he was in and the sin he was in, and this caused a lot of friction between the couple. The wife kept going to church, and the more she matured, the more she found herself attracted to Godly men. Slowly, but surely, her appetite for the "profane thing" decreased and her appetite for a God-loving, demon-slaying husband continued to increase. She spent the next few years of their marriage tagging her husband in social media posts created by Godly men, hoping that he would catch a hint and become what she was now craving. This didn't work. She also spent the next few years asking Godly men to hang out with her husband, hoping that they would rub off on him. This also proved to be ineffective, after all, he kept trying to change the Godly men. This all came to a head one Sunday during church service. That particular Sunday happened to fall on Valentine's Day, so the church was having a special service. The pastor stood to his feet and began to speak lovingly to his wife and over his wife. Without warning, he laid his hand on his wife's forehead and shouted, "The blood of Jesus covers her!" With those words, his wife fell under the power of God, and the husbands in the church began to follow suit. One by one, most of the wives fell to the floor, totally engulfed by God's love as their husbands stood over them praying. But when the woman in question looked at her husband, he was still sitting down. "Are you going to pray for me?" she asked, trying to hide the humiliation on her face. Her husband laughed and then placed his hand on her derriere. "Amen," he said before removing his hand and chuckling. "There, it's done. Now, fall out." His wife was in no way amused. Her husband had absolutely no power because he did not know Jesus, nor was he interested in getting to know Him. So, for the next few years, the wife used every tactic underneath the sun to get her husband to change his ungodly ways. It didn't work. Eventually, he met a woman who was just as carnal and ungodly as he was, if not more. He committed adultery with that woman (this is what immature people do), and after two years of going between both women, his wife finally filed for divorce. When asked why they divorced, the former couple tells people, "We grew apart." And this is true! The wife kept growing, but the husband, spiritually speaking, was a midget. In truth, the divorce represented her (the wife) divorcing a season that she had unwisely committed herself to. Think of it this way—a mother and a father walk up to their three-year old daughter at her birthday party, and they say, "We're concerned about your future. We want you to marry someone nice, so we've decided that we want you to pick out your husband today. Go outside, have the boys line up, and we want you to pick out the one that you want to marry when you turn 18-years old. The toddler whines, but does what she's told. She has all of the guys to line up, but her choice is painfully clear to everyone at the party. She can't stop laughing at the clown that had been hired to perform at her party. "Pull my finger," the clown says while standing at the back of the line. The little girl rejects his offer, while laughing hysterically. "Him!" she says, pointing at the clown. "I will marry him when I turn 18." Why did she pick the clown? Because she was too young to pick a husband for herself, he wore colorful clothing and made her laugh. During her 18th birthday party, her parents tell her to go up to her room and put on her wedding dress. She reluctantly does so, crying as she stumps her way up the steps to her bedroom. Her mother followed her into the room and asked, "What's wrong, dear? I know you're not upset about marrying Brown the Clown, after all, we didn't pick him for you. You picked him for yourself." The daughter turned around and looked at her senseless mother. "I was three, Mom! Three! I would have married a goldfish if you'd put a tux on it!" What was she saying here? In that 15-year window, her mind had changed drastically. She was no longer attracted to clowns. In other words, her mind had been transformed over the years. Utilize that same concept when it comes to picking a spouse for yourself. The man or woman you'd choose while immature isn't necessarily the person you'd choose after you've matured. This is why Matthew 6:33 tells us, "But seek ye first the kingdom of God, and his righteousness; and all these things shall be added unto you." In other words, grow up or mature before you start making adult decisions!

What did the wife do in the aforementioned story? She'd placed a period at the end of her sentence, not realizing that she would eventually outgrow that season and the relationships therein. She'd drawn a conclusion where God had placed a comma. As she began to outgrow the season she'd locked herself in, that season began to constrict her. It was like a large woman wearing a small dress. The pressure, the pain and the discomfort eventually became too much for her to bear. This is oftentimes the pressure that we erroneously refer to as warfare when it's just growing pains. The boundaries of time were now wrapped around her like a noose. Consequently, she started bursting through that period; she was thrust into a transitional phase without her permission. Again, this is the hallway between two seasons. This is the wilderness phase. The other woman was just her way of escape. God didn't send or authorize the mistress, but God allowed that window to open so that she could jump back into His will. And while in the hallway of purpose, her job was to heal, to forgive and to repent! If she refused to do either, she would be thrust back into that season to retake the tests. But this time, it would be different because the season would feel constricting. This time, she'd beg for deliverance or she'd learn to master the season she was in so that she could survive it; if this happens it is because she has no future plans of escaping it.

When you outgrow a season, you'll likely experience what feels like depression, anxiousness and a longing desire to be mentored. This is normal, and we don't necessarily have doctors and medical professionals who can fully give language to this. Most medical professionals would diagnose you with depression or anxiety. After that, they'd give you a prescription and send you home. But in many of these cases, you don't need medicine, you need mentorship. This is why Proverbs 11:14 says, "Where no counsel is, the people fall: but in the multitude of counselors there is safety." What amazes me is the fact that nowadays, we have a lot of Christians who are willing to illegally cross a few God-established boundaries just to get into or stay in a relationship, but those same people won't step foot inside of a church, won't allow themselves to be mentored and won't invest too much into books. Nevertheless, they will religiously shout, "God knows my heart!" After this, they sit around and wait year after year for God to move on their behalf, not realizing that the responsibility of movement is their own! And because they're not eating, they're not growing. They become the spiritual equivalent of that small, clay rabbit we talked about earlier that's placed in a large container. In other words, they don't have enough substance, capacity or weight to affect the seasons they're in.

Keep moving. You do this by seeking wisdom, knowledge and understanding. You do this by honoring the mentors that God brings into your life and allowing them to stretch you. And know that growing pains, while uncomfortable, are completely normal and necessary. Any believer who doesn't have spiritual stretch marks is a believer who cannot be trusted with spiritual authority.

You Were Bound to be Free

I could hear their conversation in the other room. Sarah was either very passionate or very angry—or maybe, she was passionately angry. Either way, I wasn't about to leave my room to investigate. I looked at my 13-year old son and angrily bit my lip. It was all his fault, but I couldn't be angry with him for long, after all, he'd seen the way I'd been treated over the years. He didn't like his step-mother, and he was no fan of his half-brother, Isaac, after all, she'd raised him as her own son for 14 years; that is, until she'd miraculously gotten pregnant. That's when she decided to break the news to him that she wasn't his natural mother after all. And guess what? I'm the one who had to nurse his broken heart! "Cast out this bondwoman and her son: for the son of this bondwoman shall not be heir with my son, even with Isaac!" Sarah shouted. It was becoming painfully obvious that she wanted me to hear her. She wanted her anger to become my anger; she wanted her pain to become my pain. My belly knotted up as all of her emotions tried to force their way into my heart. What about my son? What about Abraham's seed? Was she not afraid to touch God's anointed?! I walked over to Ishmael and covered his ears with my hands, but he wouldn't have it. He was around 17-years old by then, so he completely understood what was going on. He angrily removed my hands and lowered his head all the more. The tear running down his sun-kissed skin seemed to glisten under the candlelight. He was so beautiful to me, especially in that moment. Maybe it was because my motherly instincts were kicking in. Or maybe it was because I'd been so busy working for Sarah that I had neglected my own son. In that moment, I wanted to do more for him. I passionately wanted to protect him, but how?

At first, Abraham stood his ground. "No!" he shouted. Everything that he said after that wasn't audible. It was clear to me that he was trying to muffle his voice so that we couldn't hear him. At least, he had some shred of decency! I don't know what happened that night; what I do know is this—my husband, the father of my son—came into my room the next day and told me and our son to pack our things. He said that God told him to put me and his son out, but I had trouble believing this. Nevertheless, there was nothing I could do. I held back my tears because I didn't want to further upset my son. Where would we go? What would become of us?!

Note: The aforementioned is a fictitious firsthand account of Hagar's last moment in Abraham's home.

I think that most women who've read Hagar's story have found themselves upset with Sarah. First and foremost, Sarah was in a better predicament than Hagar; she was the wife of a leader and a free woman. But Hagar's story had been different. She was a slave-turned-concubine who pretty much didn't have a voice. She was significantly younger than Sarah, and even though slavery and concubinage were not frowned upon at that time, what turns the stomach of most modern-day women is the fact that Sarah told her husband to go and sleep with Hagar. In truth, we often measure this incident by what we consider normal today, and of course, in our day and age, both Sarah and Abraham would be revered as predators. But again, this is just a cultural issue. Hagar had been a bondwoman; another word for "bondwoman" is slave. And because of Sarah's jealousy and insecurities, Hagar had been tossed out of her home and sent into the wilderness to fend for herself. Then again, there is another angle that we can look at this from. Because of Sarah's insecurities and her jealousy, Hagar's walking papers were really her emancipation papers. She was no longer a bondwoman. She was a free woman, and this is something to celebrate—howbeit, how can you celebrate a freedom that you've never had? How can you celebrate a freedom that you've never asked for? Freedom, to someone in the wrong region of thought, looks and feels a lot like bondage. Hagar was accustomed to being an afterthought; she was accustomed to living in bondage, so when she'd been set free, she didn't know what to do or how she was going to survive. Genesis 21:14-21 says, "And Abraham rose up early in the morning, and took bread, and a bottle of water, and gave it unto Hagar, putting it on her shoulder, and the child, and sent her away: and she departed, and wandered in the wilderness of Beersheba. And the water was spent in the bottle, and she cast the child under one of the shrubs. And she went, and sat her down over against him a good way off, as it were a bowshot: for she said, Let me not see the death of the child. And she sat over against him, and lift up her voice, and wept. And God heard the voice of the lad; and the angel of God called to Hagar out of heaven, and said unto her, What aileth thee, Hagar? Fear not; for God hath heard the voice of the lad where he is. Arise, lift up the lad, and hold him in thine hand; for I will make him a great nation. And God opened her eyes, and she saw a well of water; and she went, and filled the bottle with water, and gave the lad drink. And God was with the lad; and he grew, and dwelt in the wilderness, and became an archer. And he dwelt in the wilderness of Paran: and his mother took him a wife out of the land of Egypt." Because she didn't know what freedom looked and felt like, Hagar had resolved within herself that both her and her son were going to die. But the scriptures tell us that God heard the voice of the young boy. God heard the prayers of Ishmael. Remember, at this point, he was between 17 to 19-years old. He wasn't a crying toddler in a poorly constructed wicker basket, as many of us have envisioned. He was a teenager, and more than that, he was the son of Abraham (the father of faith). So, it would be silly for us to think that Ishmael didn't know how to pray.

Then again, there is an angle that we all tend to avoid, and that is—Sarah had been doing her job as a wife and leader to not only protect her offspring, but to also facilitate the prophetic words that had been spoken over her son's life.

Maybe, what she'd done had been predestined before the hands of time as an event that needed to take place so that God could communicate the differences between the law versus grace; freedom versus bondage. Galatians 4:22-26 (ESV) reads, "For it is written that Abraham had two sons, one by a slave woman and one by a free woman. But the son of the slave was born according to the flesh, while the son of the free woman was born through promise. Now this may be interpreted allegorically: these women are two covenants. One is from Mount Sinai, bearing children for slavery; she is Hagar. Now Hagar is Mount Sinai in Arabia; she corresponds to the present Jerusalem, for she is in slavery with her children. But the Jerusalem above is free, and she is our mother." In other words, while Sarah's actions may appear to be immoral and insensitive to us, she was simply fanning the birds of prey away from her offering.

First and foremost, how did Hagar come to be the slave or maidservant of Sarah? She was likely one of the slaves that either Pharaoh or Abimelech gave to Abraham after he'd passed through Egypt. In both cases, Abraham had been afraid to tell the people that Sarah was his wife because of her beauty; he feared that they would kill him. Let's look at those stories.

Incident One: Genesis 12:10-20

And there was a famine in the land: and Abram went down into Egypt to sojourn there; for the famine was grievous in the land. And it came to pass, when he was come near to

115

Incident One: Genesis 12:10-20

enter into Egypt, that he said unto Sarai his wife, Behold now, I know that thou art a fair woman to look upon: Therefore it shall come to pass, when the Egyptians shall see thee, that they shall say, This is his wife: and they will kill me, but they will save thee alive. Say, I pray thee, thou art my sister: that it may be well with me for thy sake; and my soul shall live because of thee. And it came to pass, that, when Abram was come into Egypt, the Egyptians beheld the woman that she was very fair. The princes also of Pharaoh saw her, and commended her before Pharaoh: and the woman was taken into Pharaoh's house. And he entreated Abram well for her sake: and he had sheep, and oxen, and he asses, and menservants, and maidservants, and she asses, and camels. And the LORD plagued Pharaoh and his house with great plagues because of Sarai Abram's wife. And Pharaoh called Abram, and said, What is this that thou hast done unto me? why didst thou not tell me that she was thy wife? Why saidst thou, She is my sister? so I might have taken her to me to wife: now therefore behold thy wife, take her, and go thy way. And Pharaoh commanded his men concerning him: and they sent him away, and his wife, and all that he had.

Incident Two: Genesis 20:1-18

And Abraham journeyed from thence toward the south country, and dwelled between Kadesh and Shur, and

Incident Two: Genesis 20:1-18

sojourned in Gerar. And Abraham said of Sarah his wife, She is my sister: and Abimelech king of Gerar sent, and took Sarah. But God came to Abimelech in a dream by night, and said to him, Behold, thou art but a dead man, for the woman which thou hast taken; for she is a man's wife. But Abimelech had not come near her: and he said, Lord, wilt thou slay also a righteous nation? Said he not unto me, She is my sister? and she, even she herself said, He is my brother: in the integrity of my heart and innocency of my hands have I done this. And God said unto him in a dream, Yea, I know that thou didst this in the integrity of thy heart; for I also withheld thee from sinning against me: therefore suffered I thee not to touch her. Now therefore restore the man his wife; for he is a prophet, and he shall pray for thee, and thou shalt live: and if thou restore her not, know thou that thou shalt surely die, thou, and all that are thine. Therefore Abimelech rose early in the morning, and called all his servants, and told all these things in their ears: and the men were sore afraid. Then Abimelech called Abraham, and said unto him, What hast thou done unto us? And what have I offended thee, that thou hast brought on me and on my kingdom a great sin? thou hast done deeds unto me that ought not to be done. And Abimelech said unto Abraham, What sawest thou, that thou hast done this thing? And Abraham said, Because I thought, Surely the fear of God is not in this place; and they will slay me for my wife's sake. And yet indeed she is my sister; she is the daughter of my father, but not the daughter of my mother; and she

Incident Two: Genesis 20:1-18

became my wife. And it came to pass, when God caused me to wander from my father's house, that I said unto her, This is thy kindness which thou shalt shew unto me; at every place whither we shall come, say of me, He is my brother. And Abimelech took sheep, and oxen, and menservants, and womenservants, and gave them unto Abraham, and restored him Sarah his wife. And Abimelech said, Behold, my land is before thee: dwell where it pleaseth thee. And unto Sarah he said, Behold, I have given thy brother a thousand pieces of silver: behold, he is to thee a covering of the eyes, unto all that are with thee, and with all other: thus she was reproved. So Abraham prayed unto God: and God healed Abimelech, and his wife, and his maidservants; and they bare children. For the LORD had fast closed up all the wombs of the house of Abimelech, because of Sarah Abraham's wife.

In both of these incidents, Abraham had acquired menservants and maidservants. In other words, he'd acquired slaves. Hagar was likely among them. But when she had been cast out of Abraham's house, she went back into the wilderness in the direction of Egypt. In other words, she was trying to go back to the place that God had delivered her from, after all, this was all she knew. But God stopped her before she could return to her bondage. She was no longer a slave, and she needed to understand this. She was no longer a concubine, and she needed to understand this. Had she gone back to Egypt, she would have likely been returned to her former duties, along with her son.

Many of us are like Hagar. We have left behind the sin that we once knew. We were on the other side of the border—off in the land of Sin, where we enjoyed the blackberries, the blueberries, the raspberries and the strawberries. We became accustomed to being bound. As a matter of fact, we decorated our bondage with religious jargon. But one day, we were suddenly snatched out of our regions of thought and cast into the hallway of purpose. This again, is the wilderness or the space that separates one season from the other. While there, we tried to return to Sin, but the window had already closed on us, so we started sinning where we were. If we couldn't reenter Sin, we could at least recreate what we once knew. So, we sinned in the hallway, not realizing that the wilderness is designed to bring that sin to the surface so that God could cast it out of us. We cried in the hallway, we plotted our deaths in the hallway and we threw tantrums in the hallway, but none of these antics forced God to give us what we thought we wanted. Instead, He allowed us to stay in the wilderness until we finally uttered those words He'd been waiting to hear. "I surrender, Lord. Have your way. My life is not my own."

Or are you still in that hallway reminiscing about seasons-past? Are you still angry with the people who disappointed you, rejected you or mishandled you in any way? Do you understand that everything they did to the adult-sized you was partly or wholly your fault (in most cases)? Do you know that the enemy wants to keep you in a victim's mindset; this way, he can continue to attack you UNTIL you finally become what he'd decided that he wants you to be? Victims attract predators, just like Ahabs attract Jezebels or, better yet, empaths attract narcissists. You are a puzzle piece, but if you're not whole and if you haven't learned to take accountability for your role in your own hurt, you will continue to fit into the wrong pictures. To have a victim's mentality is to live in a box that's been parked in a region of thought, because you're waiting for the folks who hurt you to either:

(α) Knock on your box and apologize.

(β) Get back whatever it is that they've done to you. The world calls this "karma."

I know plenty of victims who have settled down in the wrong regions of thought. They have mastered those seasons, and consequently, they've become master manipulators, professional victims and hurt people who the devil uses to hurt people. In other words, they've never moved on. And to be fair, some people genuinely don't know how to move on, after all, they've never seen an example of a former victim-turned-overcomer. Everyone around them is a victim, master manipulator or a predator, and because of this, they've had to exchange discernment for suspicion. These people think that everyone is after them; they believe every person alive is untrustworthy, and because the seasons have closed in on them, most of them deal with health issues. The people who once robbed them of their peace have taught them to rob themselves of the futures God has set in place for them. Hagar was well on her way to becoming a professional victim. She'd gone into the wilderness on two separate occasions; the first time had been while she was pregnant with her son, Ishmael. She'd forgotten that she was a concubine, and she'd started dishonoring and mishandling her mistress, Sarah. (Again, consider the times they were in; don't read that from a modern-day perspective.) Genesis 16:5-9 reads, "And Sarai said unto Abram, My wrong be upon thee: I have given my maid into thy bosom; and when she saw that she had conceived, I was despised in her eyes: the LORD judge between me and thee. But Abram said unto Sarai, Behold, thy maid is in thy hand; do to her as it pleaseth thee. And when Sarai dealt hardly with her, she fled from her face. And the angel of the LORD found her by a fountain of water in the wilderness, by the fountain in the way to Shur. And he said, Hagar, Sarai's maid, whence camest thou? And whither wilt thou go? And she said, I flee from the face of my mistress Sarai. And the angel of the LORD said unto her, Return to thy mistress, and submit thyself under her hands." This had been the first time Hagar had gone on the run, and even then, she was trying to return to Egypt. But what did the angel of the Lord advise Hagar to do? He told her to return to the woman who had been dealing harshly with her, and to submit! How hard of a charge is this?! How do you submit to someone who has been mistreating you? It's easy! Look at how you've treated that person! Accountability is key! The Bible says that when Hagar realized she was pregnant, she'd started despising

Sarah. And sure, we can find several ways to justify Hagar's disdain for Sarah, but notice that the angel did not say that Sarah was wrong. The angel did not tell her that God was going to pay back Sarah for her sins against Hagar. Why is this?! Because God deals with us about OUR wrongs! He deals with others about THEIR OWN wrongs! This is why I raise an eyebrow towards anyone who says that God showed them what was wrong with another person. No! He told us to remove the speck from our own eyes before we try to cast it out of someone else's eyes! In other words, take inventory of your own heart! By doing this, do you realize that your forgiveness will place you on a path towards healing (and not the other way around)? By doing this, do you realize that you prove yourself to be trustworthy to God, meaning, He can upgrade your rank in the realm of the spirit? What does an upgrade look like? It looks like acceleration. What would have taken you fifteen years to acquire can and will suddenly be yours in a matter of months or minutes!

Hagar was bound to be free, and so were you. Everything that happened to you has purpose attached to it. You have a testimony; you have survived events that would have, at minimum, drove most folks crazy. And like Hagar, you may have been discounted, disregarded and written off as an irrelevant part of history, but God designed it to be this way! Remember, He uses the foolish things of this world to confound the wise! God allows some people to go into bondage just so that He can set them free. And while, there is a lot to be said about Ishmael and the theories surrounding his offspring, the fact still remains that God can, have and will save any Muslim who calls upon the name of Jesus! The blood of Jesus is for everyone who will accept Him as their Lord and Savior! Yes, you were once a bondman or a bondwoman, but through the precious shed blood of Jesus, you have been set free! Now, you have to move to another region of thought so that you can stop thinking, acting and reasoning as a slave! You have to stop being a victim so that you can step into God's promises for your life! Let's look at a few other folks who had been bound just so that God could set them free!

John 9:1-7: And as Jesus passed by, he saw a man which was blind from his birth. And his disciples asked him, saying, Master, who did sin, this man, or his parents, that he was born blind? Jesus answered, Neither hath this man sinned, nor his parents: but that the works of God should be made manifest in him. I must work the works of him that sent me, while it is day: the night cometh, when no man can work. As long as I am in the world, I am the light of the world. When he had thus spoken, he spat on the ground, and made clay of the spittle, and he anointed the eyes of the blind man with the clay, And said unto him, Go, wash in the pool of Siloam, (which is by interpretation, Sent.) He went his way therefore, and washed, and came seeing.

John 11:38-44: Jesus therefore again groaning in himself cometh to the grave. It was a cave, and a stone lay upon it.

Jesus said, Take ye away the stone. Martha, the sister of him that was dead, saith unto him, Lord, by this time he stinketh: for he hath been dead four days. Jesus saith unto her, Said I not unto thee, that, if thou wouldest believe, thou shouldest see the glory of God? Then they took away the stone from the place where the dead was laid. And Jesus lifted up his eyes, and said, Father, I thank thee that thou hast heard me. And I knew that thou hearest me always: but because of the people which stand by I said it, that they may believe that thou hast sent me. And when he thus had spoken, he cried with a loud voice, Lazarus, come forth. And he that was dead came forth, bound hand and foot with graveclothes: and his face was bound about with a napkin. Jesus saith unto them, Loose him, and let him go.

Mark 5:1-13: And they came over unto the other side of the sea, into the country of the Gadarenes. And when he was come out of the ship, immediately there met him out of the tombs a man with an unclean spirit, Who had his dwelling among the tombs; and no man could bind him, no, not with chains: Because that he had been often bound with fetters and chains, and the chains had been plucked asunder by him, and the fetters broken in pieces: neither could any man tame him. And always, night and day, he was in the mountains, and in the tombs, crying, and cutting himself with stones. But when he saw Jesus afar off, he ran and worshipped him, And cried with a loud voice, and said, What have I to do with thee, Jesus, thou Son of the most high God? I adjure thee by God, that thou torment me not. For he said unto him, Come out of the man, thou unclean spirit. And he asked him, What is thy name? And he answered, saying, My name is Legion: for we are many. And he besought him much that he would not send them away out of the country. Now there was there nigh unto the mountains a great herd of swine feeding. And all the devils besought him, saying, Send us into the swine, that we may enter into them. And forthwith Jesus gave them leave. And the unclean spirits went out, and entered into the swine: and the herd ran violently down a steep place into the sea, (they were about two thousand;) and were choked in the sea.

More:
- Moses had been bound to be set free; this way, he could facilitate the deliverance of God's people from Egypt!
- Rahab, a pagan prostitute, had been bound to be set free! Who knows the conditions that drove her into a life of shame and sin, but the truth remains that her freedom came on the heels of her helping a few of God's people to retain their freedom.
- Samson had been bound to be set free! Yes, the man had a real issue with women, but the grace of God and the power of God would not allow him to stay in bondage!
- David had been bound to be set free! He'd run for his life from Saul, but in the end, he was crowned king of Israel.
- Esther had been bound to be set free; this way, she

could aid in setting God's people free!

- Jonah had been bound to be set free! Sure, his bondage was his own doing, but God sent the fish to swallow him up so that He could set him free and use him for His glory!
- Daniel had been bound to be set free! He'd been taken to Babylon and placed in captivity! He'd been thrown in the lion's den, but God shut the mouth of the lions!
- Joseph had been bound to be set free! In the end, he served as Pharaoh's second-in-rank!
- Jacob had been bound to be set free! He served 14 years in Laban's house just to get his daughter, Rachel, but in the end, God changed his name to Israel.

This is just a short list of the people who went through the fire just to get their freedom, and their stories are still being used to help others get free thousands of years after their deaths! This is what God wants to do with your story, but remember, staying free means that you have to respect the boundaries set in place by God and by man. Being saved, sanctified and filled with the Holy Spirit doesn't mean that you are now exempt from the rules; it actually means that you are now aware of the fact that there are rules! And when you're no longer ignorant, your sins graduate from being sins of ignorance to pure rebellion, which the Lord says is as the sin of witchcraft!

OUTBREAKS AND BREAKOUTS: UNTANGLING SOUL TIES

Every human is connected to someone who's connected to someone who's connected to someone; this chain is infinite. If we were to hold hands with the people closest to us, and they were to do the same, we'd create a chain of linked hands that would stretch across the U.S. border and into every continent on the face of this planet. We're all connected somehow, someway and somewhere. What this means for us as the human race is, when one person hurts or is impacted by something, we will all feel the ripple effect of that pain at some point. Yes, even if it's four hundred years later, that domino effect will be felt by some of our descendants. 1 Corinthians 12:25-26 says, "That there should be no schism in the body; but that the members should have the same care one for another. And whether one member suffer, all the members suffer with it; or one member be honored, all the members rejoice with it." Familiarity is a close and sometimes intimate connection. It means to be linked closely, not necessarily physically, of course. There are levels of familiarity, with the strongest level being intimacy. Please note that the word "intimacy" doesn't necessarily denote sex or a romantic connection; it denotes intimate or personal knowledge. In short, the more intimate you are with a person, the more trust you'll have for that person and the more you'll know about that person. Please note that trust isn't necessarily favorable. For example, I can have an enemy who I'm familiar with, but not intimate with. This enemy can be a co-worker of mine who I've never sat down and spoken with. Our status as enemies could be the result of that co-worker feeling threatened by me because I've worked hard and started gaining traction within the organization. Let's say that I turned that co-worker in for being condescending and competitive. One day, the co-worker looks at me and says, "This isn't over." If I believe her, and I take her words as a direct threat, what I am doing essentially is trusting her. Again, trust is not always favorable. So, I could say that I know her if someone were to ask me, but this wouldn't denote an intimate connection because, in truth, I don't really personally know her. I have just seen one side of her. When I say that I know her, I'm simply saying that I recognize her face and am familiar with her to some degree.

One of the purposes of boundaries is so that we can properly arrange our connections. For example, under my computer desk right now is a bunch of wires; they are all crossed and tangled together. Anytime I'm looking for a specific cord, I have to run my fingers down that cord, pull on it and do whatever I can to trace it to the plug. I've resolved within myself plenty of times to unplug everything so that I can place those cords in order, but I haven't gotten around to it yet. Consequently, dust and debris tend to settle under those cords, so I have to lift them up whenever I'm trying to sweep under them. But there are some gadgets out there like cord covers, cable clips and cord straps that were specifically designed to address this problem. You can even use zip ties. Howbeit, I imagine that this is what many of our souls look like to God. We are so entangled in soul ties that we can't trace where our issues are coming from. So, whenever we're in the midst of an attack, we often pray about everything and everyone. What we're doing is attempting to figure out which one of these cords or soul ties the enemy is working through. All the same, we have age-old soul ties that we often don't think about because we are no longer in association with those people, nor do we think about them, but unbeknownst to us, our soul ties with them are still live wires. They are not a bunch of former connections that we are no longer impacted by. No! Many of our decisions and much of what we go through has EVERYTHING to do with who we are connected to, even if our connections with those people are no longer intimate! Please look at the chart below. Every connection on this chart represents a cord or a wire, but our hearts represent the plug. First and foremost, we must be plugged into God; He is the Source of all power. After this, everyone else has his or her proper place. But as you can see on this chart, we oftentimes tangle up our wires by putting the wrong people in the wrong spaces. Consequently, we end up with 150 live wires, all tangled up. And when some sort of ungodly power illegally enters our lives through a legal medium, we find ourselves crying out to God, trying to figure out how and why we're going through whatever it is that we're going through. And of course, the wrong order of these connections is called idolatry; it's also called disorder.

Intimacy Chart							
Correct Order	Associates/ Acquaintances	Friends	Close Friends	Extended Family	Children	Spouse	God
Out of Order	Associates/ Acquaintances	Friends	Close Friends	Extended Family	God	Children	Spouse
Out of Order	Associates/ Acquaintances	Extended Family	Friends	Spouse	Children	Close Friends	God

Exception						
Correct Order	Associates/ Acquaintances	Friends	Extended Family	Close Friends	Children	Spouse

Note: There is a friend who sticks closer than a brother.

Boundaries were designed by God to protect what's most valuable to us, and more importantly, boundaries were designed to protect systems. Everyone I'm connected to is a part of the system that fuels my life. I was speaking about this with a sister in Christ one day, but I used the word "veins" to describe our connections, rather than wires, and she said something that was really profound. She referred to each erroneous connection as a blood clot. Think about it. Sometimes, what we've been praying and asking God for cannot and has not come through to us because we have a spiritual blood clot somewhere within our systems. We like to believe that everything in our lives is a product of happenstance, and some issues are the direct results of someone else's mismanagement of us. In other words, we often relegate the responsibility of untangling our lives to someone else. It's his fault or her fault, but never our own. Because of this, we spend half of our lives stuck in seasons that we were supposed to graduate from two decades ago. Look around you. Most forty-year old men and women are still entangled in the soul ties they created in their twenties. And it is through these ungodly soul ties that the enemy is able to invade some of our cities, states or neighborhoods of thinking. He is able to advance from the romantic states that we have left in ruins fifteen years ago and into our financial states, where he proceeds to launch an attack against our finances. He keeps advancing generation after generation until someone gets enough knowledge and boldness to finally confront him. And get this, while untangling some of these wires, that person has to temporarily and sometimes permanently unplug from certain people. Whenever I decide to untangle the wires under my computer desk, I will have to unplug most, if not all of them. Next, I have to separate or classify them before placing a zip tie or cord connector around them. And finally, I have to plug them back up. After doing this, I will discover cords that should have been unplugged a long time ago, because I'm no longer using whatever it is that they are attached to.

In February of this year (2020), we saw our first few outbreaks of the Novel Coronavirus in the United States. Like most countries, our government moved swiftly to contain the virus, but to no avail. It moved through the United States like a wildfire, leaving a trail of death, destruction, grief and fear in its wake. What's interesting is the reported origins of this virus. Scientists traced it back to a bat from a live animal market in Wuhan, China. There have been a lot of theories, with the most prevalent one being that some young girl contracted the virus after eating a bowl of bat soup. Scientists have now debunked this theory, replacing it with the theory that the virus transmitted from a live bat at the wet market to a human. The following was reported by Business Insider:

> "The novel coronavirus and the SARS outbreak of 2003 have two things in common: Both are from the coronavirus family, and both have been associated with animals commonly sold in 'wet markets.' Historically at such markets, outdoor stalls are squeezed together to form narrow lanes, where locals and visitors shop for cuts of meat and ripe produce. A stall selling caged chickens may abut a butcher counter, where meat is chopped as nearby dogs watch hungrily. Some vendors hock hares, while seafood stalls display glistening fish and shrimp. Wet markets put people and live and dead animals — dogs, chickens, pigs, snakes, civets, and more — in

constant close contact. That makes it easy for zoonotic diseases to jump from animals to humans. 'Poorly regulated, live-animal markets mixed with illegal wildlife trade offer a unique opportunity for viruses to spillover from wildlife hosts into the human population,' the Wildlife Conservation Society said in a statement. In the case of SARS and the new coronavirus disease, called COVID-19, bats were the original hosts. The bats then infected other animals, which transmitted the disease to humans."

What's most intriguing is how one infected human being could indirectly touch and impact the lives of over five million people around the world, and that's just confirmed cases. I haven't even added in the number of people who've lost loved ones! This pandemic has traveled to every country and made a name for itself all around the world. Think about the people closest to you. Their pain can and does affect you. This is why God told us in Galatians 6:2, "Bear ye one another's burdens, and so fulfill the law of Christ." All the same, God can and often does end some of our relationships because of something or someone one or both of the parties' involved is connected to. This includes our pasts. Sometimes, God wants to sever the connection between you and your yesterday, but the people you're connected to won't allow this to happen, so He has to disconnect you from them. This is to stop a spiritual pandemic from taking place in your future. For example, the year was 2015 and I'd just moved to Georgia from Florida. I was still in the process of settling into my new apartment. I was also in the middle of watching a twenty-year friendship of mine take its last breath. My former friend and I hadn't argued, nor were we contentious with each other in any way. We were both just changing. We'd gone from being close friends who talked several times a day to distant friends who texted each other every now and again. Eventually, there was a month's space between our conversations, and then, three months. Finally, we started texting each other every few months. She was once a priceless fixture in my life, but sometimes, what was once a good connection can and does go bad. This doesn't mean that the person is bad; it simply means that the connection is no longer healthy. For example, I want you to imagine two cities. Now, imagine a woman in one of those cities standing at the border of that city, holding an empty can up to her ear. There is a string attached to that can, and if you follow the string with your eyes, you'll see that it leads to another city far away. On the other end of that string is another woman holding an empty can up to her ears. The cities both represent regions of thought or seasons. The string that attaches both cans or modes of communication to one another represents a soul tie. The cans represent an outdated idea or means of communication. You see, when you are seasons apart from a person, the direction of your conversation is contrary to the direction of the other person's conversation. So, you may want to talk about the future, whereas, they like to talk about the past. And I watched this unfold in a few of my own relationships. The more I healed and matured, the more excited I became about the future. My former friend wasn't an enemy when our friendship ended, and till this day, we haven't come up against each other in any way. We simply grew apart. You see, she was only a month older than me, but she acted more like a big sister to me, which was great in seasons' past. This is because I was making a lot of foolish decisions, especially with relationships, and she always had to play the referee between me and my choices, and everything that came with them. Because of this, her view of me was stunted by her experiences with me. And even though I'd changed years prior to 2015, she still kept speaking to the past me, not the woman I was. It was hard for her to accept what God was doing in and through me, so she still felt the need to speak to my past choices. Now, don't mistake what I'm saying. I'm not saying that she was a bad person; I'm saying that she was a perfect fit for the unstable Tiffany, but she no longer fit where I was at in that moment or where I was headed. So, what I had to do was put the can down and pick up a more up-to-date means of communication. I wouldn't answer the old line anymore; instead, I required that she call me on the new line. In other words, I drew boundaries around my ears and my lips; I only wanted to talk futuristically. When she spoke of the past, I started countering those conversations with talks of love, forgiveness and forward movement. I then began to pull on her potential, trying to get her out of the past because I didn't want to lose our friendship. She was someone I'd never imagined having to live without. Nevertheless, that door eventually closed and we just stopped calling each other.

Again, we didn't argue, fight or do anything to facilitate the end of our friendship. I just simply changed and I stopped hiding who I had become. You see, I was like most women who've dared to grow. I had friends who I could speak futuristically with, and with them, I could be myself without apology. So, when I spoke with them, we laughed, we talked for hours on end and we made plans for the future. But when I spoke with my former friend, I couldn't have those conversations because she would end them by bringing up the past. I remember starting to feel drained after each conversation. So again, God had me to end that mode of communication and pick up a more updated means of communication, and then, I had to require her to meet me in the future and not the past. Please understand that someone who was a great friend in times' past can be an enemy of your future if they refuse to adjust their perspective. And again, you can't write them off as bad people, after all, they helped you to get to where you are right now. That former friend of mine is the reason I have never been arrested. She's sat up late hours with me, talking me out of doing some of the silliest things, and she prayed whenever she couldn't talk me out of doing something crazy. This is why I love her and place honor on her, however, try as I may, I could not drag her into my future.

I also learned that soul ties aren't always the way we've once envisioned them to be. Like most Christians, I imagined a soul tie to be a spiritual cord that resembled an umbilical cord, so when I prayed for people, I would shout, "I sever the soul tie between _____ and _____ right now!" And while I do believe this is a temporary fix, I now understand that it's not a permanent one. Here's what I've learned—soul ties aren't spiritual ropes that serve as a bridge between two people. It's way more complicated than that. A soul tie is the mixing together of two seasons through an event called agreement. Remember, a season is nothing but a mindset; it is not a time-stamped event, even though God can and often does attach a timer to it. And get this, when you try to mix two seasons together, it creates an environment of instability, and this is what causes destructive weather to form. A soul tie, in layman's terms, is an agreement between two or more people. Keep in mind that not all agreements are entered into favorably or intentionally (more on this shortly). Soul ties are formed when:

1. We find an area in which we can relate to a person.
2. We decide to connect in that area with the intent of building something more intimate with that person.

For example, we can all relate to meeting another woman or man who we believe has the potential to be a great friend. Someone at your job, at your church or in your neighborhood walks up to you and starts chatting away. Let's say it's someone from your neighborhood. She sees you on your daily walk, and she yells across her lawn at you. "How are you? Out for another walk, I see!" You wave and respond, "Yeah, I need to get in shape! I'm trying to walk off two brownies and a slice of pizza from earlier today!" She laughs and starts walking in your direction. "Yeah, I need to start walking with you. Let me ask you something. Where did you get those shoes? I have some walking shoes in the house, but they always pinch my toes." You slow down and finally come to a complete stop because her movements and body language signal that she wants to have a conversation. What is she doing? She's trying to relate to you. If you don't show too much interest in a discussion about shoes or walking, she will hinge onto something you say in her attempt to create a connection with you. For example:

"Where did you get those shoes? I have some walking shoes in the house but they always pinch my toes."

"I honestly don't know where they came from. They were a gift. I think I got them back in 2016 from an uncle of mine who was stationed in Kuwait."

"Kuwait? Oh wow! I wish I knew somebody over there. Is he still in Kuwait?"

"No, he's in Germany now. I think he's retired from the military, but he decided to settle down in Germany."

"I heard it's nice over there! One of my cousins was in the military. She spent three years in Germany, and she loved it over there!"

"Yeah, he loves it too. He married a German woman, and they just had their third child."

"How old is he?"

"Fifty-six."

"Fifty-six and still having children?! I'm 36 and I don't want any more. If I have another one, it will be after I meet a man and get married. But right now, I don't see that happening."

"Oh wow. How many children do you have?"

"Two. My son is eight, and my daughter is twelve. You?"

"I have two boys."

"Two boys? How do you do it? I have one and he's already driving me crazy!"

"A lot of prayer, fasting and speaking in tongues."

"Amen. What church you go to?"

What do you see in the banter above? The woman is trying to connect with you. This is how friendships are formed, of course. In this dialogue, you'll notice the conversation shifting from one topic to another on several occasions. It started with the shoes, and when you mentioned an uncle in Kuwait, the neighbor hinged on those words. She obviously could not relate to talks of Kuwait, so she engaged more in the conversation about the uncle in Germany since she'd had a cousin who once lived in Germany. The conversation continued to shift until it started getting more personal. The neighbor mentioned that she had two children, stopping to say that she would potentially consider another one once she meets a man and gets married. In other words, she was indirectly telling you that she is single. Why is she sharing this? She wants to know if you're single too because she wants to see what type of connection she can form with you. Maybe, she has an opening for a close friend; this isn't a bad thing. We've all been here, and some of us are still hoping to meet one or two people who we can have close connections with. If you're married, this tells her that you won't have a lot of time to hang out, so you probably won't become a close friend; you'd be more of a distant friend (even though you live close to her) or you'd be an acquaintance. But if you're unmarried and not dating anyone, she's hoping that the two of you can become good friends. But she has to find an agreement or an area that she can either relate to you in or an area that she wants to relate to you in. So, if you have nothing in common, she may settle for being walking buddies. She'll try to pick up one of your interests like walking in an attempt to connect with you. Your job isn't to become her friend. Your job is to test that spirit (we are all spirits living in a body). This takes time, prayer and observation. In other words, she can't start off calling you her best friend or even her friend. (Some people do this when they have little to no concept of what a friend truly is.) If she starts walking with you, your job, according to the scriptures, is to guard what's intimate—your heart! So, I wouldn't tell her intimate details about my life just yet. And if she tells me too much too soon, I won't give into the temptation to reciprocate this act by telling her everything there is to know about me. You see, I need to know if this is a candidate for prayer; maybe, I'm supposed to be an evangelist to her. Maybe, I'm supposed to mentor her, or she may need to mentor me. Then again, she may be problematic. She may be a gossiper, adulteress and con artist who's looking for her next victim. She could be narcissistic, manipulative and schizophrenic. I won't know this unless I'm patient enough to test the spirit! Over time, she may become a friend or a close friend if she's mature; if not, we may become walking buddies—nothing more, nothing less.

I used to make the mistake of allowing people to prematurely refer to me as their friend, and then promote themselves by suddenly declaring that we were best friends. Those relationships almost always became one-sided. In other words, I was the giver and they were the receivers. I had to place the right labels on these relationships in order for me to stop feeling used, taken advantage of and offended. When I put the right labels on my relationships, I was able to enforce the laws associated with each label. For example, you wouldn't share information with a distant friend that you'd share with a close friend. All the same, you wouldn't be as available for a distant friend as you are for a close friend. This is why some people rush relationships by referring to you as their best friend about two weeks into your friendship. It's okay to say to someone, "I don't know you enough to call you my friend or my best friend. We're building a friendship right now, and I think you're an amazing person. I hope that we do grow to be friends, but let's not rush anything." You see, in our day and age, this statement is culturally unacceptable because we're so used to brandishing labels and sticking them onto everything and everyone who triggers an emotional response from us. I often use this analogy—imagine that you've purchased a box filled with can goods. There are 24 cans in the box; eight of them contain chopped carrots, eight contain corn and the remaining eight contain green peas. But there are no labels on the cans. One day, you find yourself craving corn, but you don't know which can has corn in it. You try shaking them all, but this doesn't help you much, so you take a gamble—you open a can. To your dismay, you find yourself staring at a bunch of green peas. You are highly disappointed because you opened the can looking for one thing, but found another. Now, imagine that you went and purchased a bunch of blank labels; you wrote "corn" on some, "peas" on some and "carrots" on the others. You do the shake test again, and you're sure that you know what's in each can. You label all the cans and put them away. The next day, you decide to pair your baked chicken up with some corn, so you grab one of the cans that says "corn." You open the can, and to your dismay, you find yourself staring at a bunch of chopped carrots. You'd be disappointed because you placed the wrong label on that particular can. This would cause you to distrust every other can in your cabinet because you clearly missed the mark on that one. This is similar to what we do in friendships. We often place the wrong labels on the people in our lives simply because we had a few good conversations with them, but when the time comes for them to live up to the labels we've placed on them, we end up disappointed, offended and hurt. This causes us to distrust everyone else in our lives, and any time you don't trust a person, you won't be fair to that person. Let's look at the story of Jacob and Esau.

> "And it came to pass, that when Isaac was old, and
> his eyes were dim, so that he could not see, he called
> Esau his eldest son, and said unto him, My son: and

he said unto him, Behold, here am I. And he said, Behold now, I am old, I know not the day of my death: Now therefore take, I pray thee, thy weapons, thy quiver and thy bow, and go out to the field, and take me some venison; And make me savoury meat, such as I love, and bring it to me, that I may eat; that my soul may bless thee before I die.

And Rebekah heard when Isaac spake to Esau his son. And Esau went to the field to hunt for venison, and to bring it. And Rebekah spake unto Jacob her son, saying, Behold, I heard thy father speak unto Esau thy brother, saying, Bring me venison, and make me savory meat, that I may eat, and bless thee before the LORD before my death. Now therefore, my son, obey my voice according to that which I command thee. Go now to the flock, and fetch me from thence two good kids of the goats; and I will make them savory meat for thy father, such as he loveth: And thou shalt bring it to thy father, that he may eat, and that he may bless thee before his death. And Jacob said to Rebekah his mother, Behold, Esau my brother is a hairy man, and I am a smooth man: My father peradventure will feel me, and I shall seem to him as a deceiver; and I shall bring a curse upon me, and not a blessing. And his mother said unto him, Upon me be thy curse, my son: only obey my voice, and go fetch me them. And he went, and fetched, and brought them to his mother: and his mother made savory meat, such as his father loved. And Rebekah took goodly raiment of her eldest son Esau, which were with her in the house, and put them upon Jacob her younger son: And she put the skins of the kids of the goats upon his hands, and upon the smooth of his neck: And she gave the savory meat and the bread, which she had prepared, into the hand of her son Jacob. And he came unto his father, and said, My father: and he said, Here am I; who art thou, my son? And Jacob said unto his father, I am Esau thy firstborn; I have done according as thou badest me: arise, I pray thee, sit and eat of my venison, that thy soul may bless me. And Isaac said unto his son, How is it that thou hast found it so quickly, my son? And he said, Because the LORD thy God brought it to me. And Isaac said unto Jacob, Come near, I pray thee, that I may feel thee, my son, whether thou be my very son Esau or not. And Jacob went near unto Isaac his father; and he felt him, and said, The voice is Jacob's voice, but the hands are the hands of Esau. And he discerned him not, because his hands were hairy, as his brother Esau's hands: so he blessed him. And he said, Art thou my very son Esau? And he said, I am. And he said, Bring it near to me, and I will eat of my son's venison, that my soul may bless thee. And he brought it near to him, and he did eat: and he brought him wine, and he drank. And his father Isaac said unto him, Come near now, and kiss me, my son. And he came near, and kissed him: and he smelled the smell of his raiment, and blessed him, and said, See, the smell of my son is as the smell of a field which the LORD hath blessed: Therefore God give thee of the dew of heaven, and the fatness of the earth, and plenty of corn and wine: Let people serve thee, and nations bow down to thee: be lord over thy brethren, and let thy mother's sons bow down to thee: cursed be every one that curseth thee, and blessed be he that blesseth thee."

The blessing of the firstborn was a rite of passage for the firstborn son, and Jacob stole it from his brother by deceiving his father. In order for Jacob to steal this blessing, he had to pretend to be his brother. The message here is—for every label, there is a certain amount of access to a particular area of your life. Someone who is only mature enough to be a distant friend can and will often refer to you as his or her best friend if that person sees something in your life that he or she wants access to. For example, if you're heavily into fitness, someone who wants a personal coach but can't afford one may start referring to you as a friend. Three weeks later, she may call you her best friend, using the fact that she has shared some details about her childhood with you that she's never shared with anyone else. She's not a friend; she's a mentee or a client, and if you don't put the right label on that relationship, you will inevitably be used and feel used. Consequently, you'll spend several months or years stuck in a region of thought because of, not necessarily who you are connected to, but how you are connected to that person. Again, not all soul ties are entered into favorably or intentionally, for example, a woman uses manipulation to seduce another woman's husband when he is in a season of weakness. (Note: this can and does happen.) His mother has passed away, he'd been terminated from his job, and one of his stepsons has been rebelling against him and every other authority figure. To make matters worse, his wife is far too self-absorbed to acknowledge her husband's pain or even minister to him. This doesn't mean she's a bad person; the issue is that their relationship started in the wrong region of thought. Mark (the husband) had always given Natalie (his wife) anything she'd wanted, even when he knew it was not in "their" best interest. Nevertheless, he hated to see his wife pouting, and even more, he hated for her to be upset with him, so for 18 years, Mark spoiled Natalie, often explaining away his passivity with, "Happy wife, happy life." But now, for the first time in their marriage, he needs her, but she genuinely doesn't know how to be there for him because this has never been a requirement. So, while her husband is ailing away, Natalie utilizes that time to shop, and she even makes the mistake of asking Mark how long he was going to "be that way," meaning, how long was he going to mourn. Her insensitivity and inability to empathize with him has caused him to enter another level of mourning—one that she is unaware of. While mourning his mother, he also unknowingly begins to mourn his marriage.

One day, Mark stopped at the post office to check his mailbox. This is a daily trend for him; it's something he does immediately after he gets off work. And he has always run into a beautiful woman there by the name of Ann. Ann is a widowed, 39-year old woman with twin daughters, both of whom have just gone away to college. Like Mark, Ann has a habit of going to the post office after work every day to check her mailbox, and she almost always runs into Mark. In truth, Ann intentionally waits until 4:45 to go to the post office because she wants to run into Mark. Her job lets out at 4:00, and she works five minutes away from the post office, so she lounges around her job every day until 4:30. She then leaves and makes her way to the post office, where she sits in her car for five minutes, reading her text messages and checking her social media pages. At exactly 4:45, she gets out of her car and walks into the post office.

While at the post office, Mark ran into Ann once again, and as always, the two of them greeted one another. Ann has always found Mark to be an attractive man, but she also knew that he was married, after all, she'd sneaked a peak at his ring finger and saw his wedding band several months prior to that day. And Ann isn't a bad person, but she is broken. We equate the word "broken" with "bad," and this often leads us to unforgiveness, but that's another message. I will say this—broken people do bad things because it's all they know.

"Again, Mr. Hanes, my condolences! And don't forget what I said! Take it one day at a time! Call me if you need me! We all need somebody," one of the post office workers shouted as Mark walked towards the exit door. That's when Ann interrupted.

Ann: Condolences? Are you okay?

Mark: Yeah, I recently lost my mother to Alzheimer's, but I'm okay. One day at a time, right?

Ann: Right. I completely understand.

Mark: And that's Mr. Jones. He's always trying to get me to talk about it.

Ann: Yeah, sure, but we all need someone to talk to every now and again. I lost my mother to Alzheimer's three years ago, and recently, I lost my husband as well. He was in the Army—he had been stationed in Iraq. Someone threw a bomb at his jeep, and just like that, I became a widow.

Mark: Oh wow, I'm sorry to hear that. Are you okay? How have you been holding up?

Ann: Thanks, I'm getting through it, but I shared that to make a point. I didn't have the help I needed after my mother passed away. Everyone sees me as strong, so they kinda just let me grieve on my own. And when my husband passed, I was so caught up in making sure our daughters had everything they needed for college that I honestly forgot to grieve. I ended up having a nervous breakdown and had to be hospitalized for nearly a week. So, make sure you grieve. Get some counseling, get some hugs—listen, get whatever you need.

Mark: Thanks! What are the symptoms of a nervous breakdown, if you don't mind me asking?

Ann: Well, I started having nervous twitches. I was depressed, but I just didn't know it because I was too busy to process my emotions. I also became very moody, and I started fantasizing about taking my life. It all came to a head the day I'd had a panic attack while at work. They made me go to the hospital, and while there, they told me I'd had a nervous breakdown.

Mark: I've definitely had a few involuntary twitches, but nothing major.

Ann: Don't wait for it to get worse. Here. Take my number if you're not comfortable going to a doctor, and you can talk to me. I'll help you the way my therapist helped me.

Mark: That's nice of you, but ...

Ann: Listen, I know you're married. Your wedding ring gave you away. I'm not trying to hook up with you. I'm just trying to help you the way I needed someone to help me. Here, let me start with this—a hug.

With that, Ann crossed another boundary. She wrapped her arms around Mark and gave him one of the tightest hugs he'd ever had. It felt so good to him! Three days later, he finally gave in and called Ann around ten that evening. His wife had fallen sound asleep after complaining about him not cooking every Tuesday like he normally did. Frustrated, disgusted and hurt, Mark called Ann to just talk about his fears. "What if my mother is in hell?" he asked. "I'm Christian and so was my mother, but she didn't live a saved life." Mark was feeling vulnerable at that moment. Normally, he was super masculine, but on that day, all of his emotions had finally piled up on him until he couldn't hold back anymore. Ann reassured him that his mother was in Heaven looking down on him. She was so very strong, knowledgeable, patient and selfless—she was everything that Natalie was not. Before long, Mark had entered into an emotional affair with Ann, sharing things with her about himself that he'd never shared with Natalie. He'd already begun mourning his marriage, and now, he was in the process of creating a soul tie with Ann. Three months later, the two of them met up for drinks, and two hours later, they found themselves at Ann's house dancing the night away. They woke up lying next to each other the next day, reminiscing about the passionate night they'd shared. Was this an act of premeditation? Partly. It was on Ann's behalf, but not on Mark's. Now, it eventually graduated to premeditation when he'd opened his heart to her. This is what allowed the soul tie or agreement to form between Mark and Ann. And his soul tie with her was far stronger than the one he'd had with his wife. Why is this? How could he throw 18 years of marriage away for a woman he met several months ago? Consider this concept—a man driving a Dodge Ram has the job of pulling around a small school bus every day. This has put a lot of strain on his truck. One day, his boss comes to him and says, "We're going to let the bus stay parked for a few months, so for April, May, June and some of July, I just want you to pull that Volkswagen Beetle over there." It wasn't the best-looking car, but it was definitely a lot less stressful for the guy to manage and a whole lot easier to pull. Now, imagine that the time comes for him to choose between pulling that bus around versus continuing to pull the Volkswagen around. Which one do you think he's going to choose? The weight from the bus put a lot of strain, wear and tear on the chains used to pull that bus, just like it put a lot of strain, wear and tear on the guy's vehicle. And there, you have it! This is why it was easy for him to throw 18 years away. His wife was this bus, but Ann felt a lot like a Volkswagen Beetle. Of course, he would soon discover that the Volkswagen is attached to 18 other vehicles, all of which he will soon find himself pulling around. It's the small foxes that destroy the vine. I didn't say that it was wise, after all, he'd created a culture in his marriage that did not serve him and his wife as a unit; it only served his wife, so he's more to blame for the destruction of his marriage than his wife is. Mark's soul tie with Ann had been entered in through trauma. He was in a season of trauma, and because she'd been there before, Ann knew how to reach him, empathize with him and give him the support and nurturing he needed while in that season. Once he's healed, their soul tie would likely begin to weaken; that is, unless another traumatic event took place or they continued to bond over his grief. In other words, if he wants to keep Ann, he would have to remain in that region of thought. They would have to build their relationship on the foundation of grief; they would have children on the foundation of grief, and they would end up breaking up once one of them got tired of being stuck in that place and decided to move on.

There are many doors and windows that allow for soul ties to form, and one of those doors is called trauma. Trauma is like a dent in the soul that disables it from functioning (thinking) properly. But just like a dent in a vehicle, it can be pulled out if the right tools are used, especially during sensitive moments. Manipulation can pull that dent out, but it puts a dent in another area of our lives. In Mark's case, it put a dent in his marriage, in his reputation and in his soul—one that will ultimately affect his bloodline. His sons will likely follow in his footsteps, and his daughters may find themselves attracted to men just like him. Consequently, they will marry in the regions of thought that they were raised in; this is so they can prove their loyalty to the people in those regions of thought and they can marry men and women who they can relate to. The untold truth is—some people are married to certain seasons or regions of thought. In other words, they are committed to a mindset that God only wanted them to pass through. Newsflash—you don't have to be loyal to the ditch you were born in, especially if that pit was designed to ensnare you! This is why some people happily refer to themselves as "ghetto" or as "rednecks." They are proudly stuck in seasons that are no longer beneficial for them! Howbeit, they are often rewarded by the citizens of those regions of thought. What is the reward? They are called "real ones" and given the right hand of fellowship or, better yet, the respect of the crabs who refuse to come out of the bucket.

Trauma isn't always the result of an unforeseen and

uncontrollable event. Sometimes, it is the product of our poor choices. For example, Mark made a poor choice when he'd decided to be a passive participant in his own marriage. He made an even worse choice when he decided to have an affair with Ann. These choices form cords, all of which will serve to entangle and imprison his soul all the more. Let's say that he leaves his wife and marries Ann. First and foremost, divorcing his wife won't sever the soul tie; it only creates a tangled connection between her and every other woman he ties himself to. For three years, his marriage to Ann is heavenly. She's understanding, selfless, charismatic and a whole lot of fun to be around. But one growing issue that they have is in the form of an ex-turned-friend who Ann refuses to fully disconnect from. Not wanting to look insecure, Mark tolerates Ricardo, mainly because he has a live-in girlfriend and two children with her. Nevertheless, Ricardo is a very present and very active force in Ann's life, often calling or texting her every day or every other day. Mark has questioned his new wife about her "friend," but those discussions have always turned sour, so he had resolved within himself to just be watchful, but silent. After a series of questionable events, including finding a condom wrapper in Ann's shoe, Mark finally gets the confirmation he needs when Ricardo's girlfriend suddenly shows up at their home looking for Ann. Mark told Zuri that his wife wasn't home, and what Zuri said next caused his world to come crashing down on him, burying all doubts that he'd had. "I know she's not home. She's out with my husband, Ricardo! I came home early from work today and caught them in my

bed together! I tried to beat the dust out of your wife, but Ricardo got between us. She ran out of our house naked, and Ricardo ran behind her when he saw me heading towards the gun cabinet. They got in Ricardo's car ... I'm assuming he had to take her to wherever she'd parked her car!" Mark and Zuri talked for about 15 minutes before Ann pulled into the driveway. When she saw Zuri, she tried to back out, but the cops pulled up behind her car. As it turned out, Zuri had already called the police and reported a crime in progress, saying that she was about to go to Ann's house and kill her. Of course, Mark and Ann eventually end up divorcing and Mark is all the more traumatized. But he still isn't free! He's still entangled in the soul tie, not just with Ann but also with Natalie and every other woman in his past; that is, until he leaves those regions of thought. Let's say that he reaches out to me and says, "I'm tired of thinking about Ann! I'm tired of wondering who she's with, how happy she is and how miserable I am! I want this soul tie to break! Can you do one of those soul tie prayers so I can move on, please?!" (I normally don't get these types of messages from men, but I do often get them from women). One of the lessons I had to learn was that, while praying for soul ties to break off of people's lives, I needed to also point them in the direction of:
1. a counselor or therapist
2. a mentor
3. a pastor (if they didn't have one)
4. a book
5. repentance
6. God, above all else

Their minds needed to change. They didn't need spiritual warfare, they needed information, transformation, and most of all, they needed to repent! I had to stop praying deliverance prayers over folks who simply needed a book, a therapist and to have a conversation with God!

Let's revisit the topic of pandemics. One woman, one bat and one bad decision led to millions of people fighting for their lives. Lives have been lost, economies have been destroyed, families have been ripped apart and countries are threatening to go into a cold war all because of one woman's decision. I'm not saying that what she did was wrong, after all, it was culturally acceptable. What I am saying is that her decision cost a lot of people their lives. Now, I want you to take that information and relate it to soul ties. The average person has been touched by far more people than you know, and I'm not talking about physically, I'm talking about mentally. Let's use Mark and Ann as an example. Mark is soul tied to his wife, Natalie. He created an emotional soul tie with Ann, and that soul tie strengthened the day he had sex with her. But what Mark didn't know was that Ann was also soul tied to seven other guys who were each soul tied to, at minimum, twenty women each; this isn't counting the four other guys Mark's wife was soul tied to, all of which were connected to, at minimum, fifteen other women each. All the same, Mark was still soul tied to thirty women from his past. Can you count the bodies in this equation? That's more than 240 bodies in one bed! And we're not adding the body counts these people's exes have built up! Do you see how a sexually transmitted disease can cross the borders of India, make its rounds around Europe two hundred times before stopping off in Africa, and then, making its way to your small city in America, only to find itself knocking on your window at three in the morning? What was once foreign to your life can easily become a familiar presence. We're all connected, and I think COVID-19 is a painful reminder of this. The AIDS pandemic should have been a painful reminder, and while it was a wake up call for many, some people are still acting like it doesn't exist!

An outbreak is the result of people being connected in the wrong way. Sometimes, these connections are seasonal connections that we neglect to remove ourselves from. It makes me think of chicken. If I buy a pack of raw chicken and place it in my refrigerator, I only have so much time before I have to cook that chicken. If the expiration date passes, the chicken will begin to decompose. So, while it may have been a good deal and while it had the potential to be a great meal, if it's not utilized in its proper season, it then becomes toxic. To stop an outbreak, you have to break out of the mindset or agreement that you and the other person are meeting up in. Sometimes, we're simply connected to the right people in the wrong way.

Many of our relationships with people are like this. We have a great financial relationship with them, but our personal relationships with them is toxic. Consequently, what keeps crossing out of their lives into our lives is literally killing us! Again, it is possible to be connected to the right person in the wrong way. For example, I could come across a guy like Mark (from the aforementioned story) at the post office, and God could give me a simple assignment—that is to encourage him in that moment only. After that, my job would be to connect him to a man of God at my church—right there on the spot! That's all! Not give him my phone number and promise to connect them later. So, my connection to him could be ordained for a moment, but if I started creating another connection with him, I'd be connected to the right assignment in the wrong way, even if I simply became his friend. This is because he's wounded in the area of romance, and it would be easy for me to turn his heart away from his wife; yes, even unintentionally. This would essentially cause our relationship to become demonic. In other words, our soul tie or the meshing together of our minds would provide the enemy with the opportunity he wants to transmit something ungodly from me to Mark or from Mark to me. So, if I'm wrestling with lust and adultery, a soul tie would provide Satan the bridge he needs to finish off Mark's marriage.

When you marry the borders of two hearts together, the lines become blurry, and no one knows where they start and where the other person ends. This is what we call intimacy. Intimacy is the process of becoming one with another person or spirit. In truth, there are marriages on life support today because of forty-year old soul ties that have never been addressed. For example, I'd met a man who we'll call Duke when I was 18-years old and broken. When I was 38 years old, he reached back out to me. He was still soul-tied to the old me, even though I wasn't soul-tied to him. (I tell people all the time that it is possible to be a part of a one-sided soul tie. Most people have them with their favorite celebrities, but I digress.) After Duke reached out to me, he told me that he was going through a divorce. He'd been married for twenty years! That's two decades! But he also shared with me that he'd thought of me and dreamed of me often over the years. Some would argue that he was probably trying to coerce me into a sexual relationship. And while this could be true, I can wholeheartedly say that I knew he was being transparent. He reminded me of events and conversations that I had totally forgotten about. He was still smitten, and I could hear it, but by smitten, I don't mean that he loved me. No! I wasn't even in the least bit deceived! That's not love, and I had learned this over the course of my life! He was soul-tied to a corpse; he was still connected to the dead version of me, and those seducing spirits that used me to bind him back in 1995 or 1996 still had cords wrapped around his mind. This is why I spoke to those cords and commanded them to break! I also addressed his belief system, telling him the truth, and that was—I had never loved him. I was a broken woman looking for attention. I was nice about it, but there's no kind-enough way to tell someone something they don't want to hear, especially if they've believed otherwise for as long as he had. But my assignment in that moment wasn't to spare his feelings, it was to set him free. All the same, the truth can only set you free if you embrace it.

This brings me to my last point. You can have a stronger

soul tie with a person than they have with you. Let's deal with this on a gender scale. Women tend to wear their hearts on their sleeves, and many men have exploited this. The Bible warns us to guard our hearts, but a lot of Western women have never learned HOW to do this. They simply know that they are supposed to guard their hearts, but not necessarily how to guard their hearts. Consequently, a man looking to bed a woman can easily appeal to her voids by just simply listening to her! All he has to do is say all the right things and let her talk. Most men know this. When you open up your heart in an event called transparency, you begin to create a one-sided soul tie with the person you're sharing with through an event called intimacy. If that person does not open up to you or shares information that is not so intimate with you, your soul tie with him or her will continue to be one-sided. And while I am a huge fan of open and healthy communication, you should NEVER open up too much too soon! Women who do this often find themselves in one-sided soul ties or in imbalanced soul ties, whereas, they are more connected with the men they're dating than those men are connected with them. The heart is comprised of several compartments, including a compartment where sensitive information is stored. If you open that compartment, you are essentially being intimate with the person you're opening up to, and this will allow a soul tie to form between you and that person. But again, it can potentially be a one-sided soul tie. In the business world, we often say, "A good businessman or businesswoman knows when to count his or her losses." I've had to learn some pretty expensive lessons over the last decade as an entrepreneur. I've invested in programs, software and people, only to not receive a return on my investment. I had to write it off as a loss and a lesson. Anytime you keep throwing something valuable into a pit and you're not getting a return on it, your effort is referred to as gambling. A gambler will sit at a slot machine for hours on end and keep throwing money into the machine, fearing that the moment he or she gets up and walks away, the next player will yield a return from that machine. Most people deal with this same fear in relationships! A woman can be yoked up with an abusive, narcissistic cheater, and she will hold on to him, fearing that the minute she leaves, he'll become everything she's ever wanted in a man, but he'll be that for someone else. So, she gambles with her sanity, staying in that relationship, arguing with a broken soul. In truth, she does more damage to the guy than she realizes, even if she is a "good" woman.

Again, one of the most common prayer requests I used to get from women was this—"Can you pray and ask God to sever the soul tie between _____ and me?! He has moved on with his life, and I'm still over here hurting! I don't want to be connected with him anymore! I want to move on!" But here's the problem with this. If the woman in question doesn't change her mind, the soul tie remains connected, because it's not some soft-tissue cord that's connecting their hearts; it's two minds meeting in a certain region of thought! In other words, they are relative to one another or, better yet, on an equal plane with one another. In layman's terms, they have found a way to relate, and anyone you start relating to, you essentially form a relationship with. If she wants to get out of that soul tie, she has to change her mind, and this can and does take time, effort and lots of information—just like it took time, effort and information to enter! Imagine her living in a house with the guy after they've broken up. Imagine her then complaining about having to share a bathroom with him, complaining about him eating food that belonged to her and complaining about him talking to other women. You'd advise her to move, right?! It would be asinine for her to continue living with him after they split up! The same is true for severing an ungodly soul tie. She would have to move on! No, she shouldn't date someone else while she's in that region of thought. She needs to repent; in other words, she needs to change her mind or the way that she thinks! This is how she divorces that season of her life! If her mind isn't changed, her heart simply becomes numb, and most women mistake this for healing, but it's just desensitization. She will then proceed to date the same demon in a different man; that is, until she gets the information she needs, ingests it and allows God to move her to a new region of thought! If she doesn't change her mind, she then becomes a professional victim/master manipulator who's bound by blame, shame and pride. Remember, victims naturally attract predators (think food chain), so she'll keep attracting predatory men, all the while, preying on them in, for example, their financial districts. But when they hurt her, she won't focus or even be cognizant of her own wrongs; instead, she will return to the role that she knows best, and that is being a victim. We see this everyday in America! And she will be so natural in that role that most people will see her as a sweet, innocent and harmless woman who's had a string of bad luck with men. Nay! She's a broken woman who refuses to change her mind! She refuses to break out of that mindset, and consequently, she keeps dealing with the same crap in a different toilet. When you refuse to break out of a mindset, you simply cannot and will not break out of a soul tie.

Every boundary that we violate has something to do with who we are connected to, how we are connected to them, and lastly, why we are connected to them. Eve sinned against God when she opened herself up to Satan while in the Garden of Eden. He'd asked her a question—"Did God actually say, 'You shall not eat of any tree in the garden'?" It was okay for her to answer this question, but the minute he said something contrary to what God had already spoken, she should have ended that conversation. Did she know that he was an enemy of God? If so, she shouldn't have spoken with him at all. Prior to this event, one third of Heaven's angels had fallen because they'd connected to Lucifer in the wrong way. And by connection, I mean they allowed him to create a void that they didn't have by causing them to want something that they did not need (to be like God). All of man's issues are because of who he or she is connected with or how he or she is connected to that person! It started off (for many of us) with our families. We had to wrestle with some generational demons and some demonic systems that had become the norm for our predecessors. Our souls were so mingled and mangled that we found ourselves connecting to any and every person who looked like they could give us the love and the answers that we so hungered for. But they just weaved themselves into our already entangled lives and messed us up all the more! We found ourselves being roped in soul tie after soul tie until we woke up one day with three children and a pending court case. The pain, the questions, the frustration, the dreams—it was all too much! Why was it so difficult to get the lives we wanted? After all, our dreams weren't that complicated or elaborate. So, we formed one soul tie in an attempt to get out of another soul tie, but this only served to entangle us all the more. And we didn't just do this in our romantic states, we did this with friends, jobs and in pretty much every area of our lives. Let's look at the relational chart.

State, City, Neighborhood	Interpretation	Type
Mentality	State of Mind	State
Physicality	State of Being	State
Spirituality	State of Faith	State
• Religiosity or Piety	State of Religion	City
Familiarity	Familial State	State
• Parenthood	State of Parenting or Being a Parent	Hood or Neighborhood of Thinking

• Brotherhood/Sisterhood	Friend State/Ability to Relate	Hood or Neighborhood of Thinking
• Romanticism	Erotic State/Romance	City
• Sexuality	Sexual State	City
Livelihood	Career State	State
• Prosperity/Poverty	State of Financial Being	City

All of these make up the system that we call living. Life is the force or the energy that animates our bodies; it is the breath of God. Living, on the other hand, is what we do with that energy. We all have dreams, fantasies and desires. Most humans simply want a nice house in a safe, orderly neighborhood, a spouse who genuinely and wholeheartedly loves them, obedient, level-headed children, financial stability, loyal friends, loving family members, a doctrinally sound church, and last but definitely not least, a relationship with God. If we had all of these things, most of us would be satisfied—or, at least, we think we'd be satisfied. In truth, all of those desires are great, but many of them are the products of voids. Remember, a void is the absence of revelation or information in any given area of our lives. To be whole means to be filled with the presence of God in every area of our lives; it means to lack nothing. Voids create hunger in the soul, and when we don't know, not what, but Who we're hungry for and why we're hungry for Him, we try to appease those voids using any and everything that we can rope in. Consequently, we start using people and anything that we can find as void-fillers. If I had everything but a sound mind as it relates to friendship, I would have a void in my brotherhood/sisterhood state. A void is darkness; it represents a hollow and empty space in my soul. Because that space has no revelation, chances are, I would be bound by a demonic entity in that area. Consequently, I'd be great at everything except being a friend. To remedy this, God would send sound people into my life to speak into that area of my soul. So, I could meet a woman who is similar to me in the area of finance or she may be someone I look up to in that area. To look up to her means that she has advanced beyond me in that particular state. I may find myself drawn to her because of how good she is at managing her money, earning more money and making sound, financial decisions. And while she's mentoring me in that area, we may find other areas that we can relate in. Over time, a friendship may start to form, but as soon as this happens, I'd prove myself to be inapt in that particular area. Her job isn't to judge me, to walk away or to talk about me. Her job is to make an impartation in that area, but before she does this, she has to count the cost. What this means is, she has to decide whether she believes that I am worth the investment (time, effort, frustration). After all, she may come across a strongman in that area. I could be bound by hurt, rejection and abandonment in that area. In other words, she needs two strengths to take on this challenge—information and patience. A stronghold is a cycle; it is a fixed system within a system, so whenever you take on the role of coming against a stronghold, you must be prepared. It's familiarizing yourself with a system of thinking so that you can dismantle it. It's learning the many fears, excuses and devils that you are going to run into while trying to help someone else. This is what makes you a specialist in that arena. Not only would she have to count the cost, she'd have to get past a common guarding spirit by the name of fear. She would have to muscle her way past her fear of confrontation so she could confront that area of my thinking. She can't fear losing me as a potential friend, she can't fear losing my respect, and she can't fear having an uncomfortable conversation with me. Another example is the Jezebel-Ahab or narcissist/empath relationship. I've sat across from friends and couples who fit this description. In this duo, one person had a Jezebel spirit, while the other person was an empath. I've listened to the empath talk nonstop about the narcissist's controlling ways, manipulations and threats. I've watched narcissists sit at the table and begin to spin their webs of deceit, trying to entangle me in those webs so that I could see the issue from their points of view. And to both of their chagrin, I didn't give too much attention to the narcissist/Jezebellic personality. I focused mostly on the empathic/Ahab personality. This is because the Jezebel spirit or narcissist (whichever you prefer) is impotent without the Ahab spirit or empath. Jezebel, in the Bible, had no real authority, except for the authority that Ahab had given her by making her queen AND by not acting as the authority figure of his home or the authority figure over the kingdom of Israel. Ahab, in modern-day terminology, was a coward. By addressing the empath, I was addressing the root of the issue. If the empath regained his or her confidence, stopped being fearful and stopped being codependent, the narcissist would either shape up or ship out. In most cases, they'll walk away because the narcissist/Jezebel personality absolutely HAS to be worshiped; that is, unless the person gets deliverance and fights to remain free. James 4:7 says it this way, "Submit yourselves therefore to God. Resist the devil, and he will flee from you." People who are bound by the Ahab spirit have relinquished their authority in exchange, in most cases, for peace. Elizabeth could be a mess in her financial state, but because she doesn't want to deal with the stress associated with working a full-time job, getting up early in the morning or dealing with people, she may opt to live with her Jezebellic mother instead, allowing her to take full financial responsibility for Elizabeth's needs. Consequently, Elizabeth may find herself being emotionally, mentally and even physically abused by her mother, BUT all of her financial needs are being met because her mother pays for everything. Elizabeth may decide that she wants her and her mother to go to counseling. If they sat across from me, the counseling session would likely be short. I'd tell Elizabeth to get a job, move out of her mother's house, set some boundaries (once she moved out), and then, I could truly counsel the two of them. Chances are, Elizabeth would be the one who requested and paid for a counseling session; her mother would just show up, hoping that the counselor would see things from her vantage point. Both people would leave the session disappointed.

1. Elizabeth would be disappointed because she hoped that I'd hear her countless stories of abuse and mistreatment, and side with her. And while I do not condone or support abusive treatment, the first cause of action would be for Elizabeth to remove herself from that situation. She would have to deal with her fears of living independent of her mother. All the same, she would have to learn to take full financial responsibility for herself. Most people bound by the Ahab spirit DO NOT want to hear this, so they'll go from counselor to therapist to pastor to family friend, looking for someone to tell them what they want to hear. Most empaths and narcissists who seek counseling don't look for information, they look for confirmation.

2. Elizabeth's mother would be disappointed the moment I acknowledged that she was problematic. By telling her daughter to leave her home, set some boundaries, and then, enforce those boundaries, I would be telling her (in her mother's view) to fully disassociate from her. Most narcissists don't see anything wrong with their behavior. They love to keep their empaths dependent on them; this is so that the empath cannot walk away. Instead, they have to rely on the narcissist. So, her mother would highlight the fact that Elizabeth is lazy, disrespectful and manipulative. They both are. Nevertheless, I learned a long time ago that it is difficult (and sometimes impossible) to counsel a Jezebel who has an Ahab in

her possession. People who have this spirit are more susceptible to counseling when they have no one to manipulate or control. In other words, they become unemployed Jezebels on the waiting list for an Ahab. This is normally when they start realizing how problematic they are.

Again, if Elizabeth truly wants to be free, she would have to count the cost and be willing to pay the price of taking back her authority. Deliverance is not for the passive; it's for the violent. Matthew 11:12 reads, "And from the days of John the Baptist until now the kingdom of heaven suffereth violence, and the violent take it by force." But don't look up at the sky and imagine robbing the heavenlies. That's not what this scripture means! Luke 17:21 says, "Neither shall they say, Lo here! Or, lo there! For, behold, the kingdom of God is within you." The Kingdom of Heaven and the Kingdom of God are used interchangeably; in other words, they mean the same thing! Jesus said that the Kingdom of Heaven suffers violence and the violent take it by force. He also said that the Kingdom of God is within us. In other words, you have to violently pull your potential out of yourself! The same would be true for Elizabeth. If she's not desperate enough, she'd be wasting my time, her mother's time and her own time by setting up counseling sessions. After all, you can't counsel dysfunction. You can't talk a demon out of being a demon. All the same, she's not wanting to get counseling where she needs it the most; instead, she'd be essentially asking me to tell her mother to stop arguing, complaining and playing mind games so that she could leach off her mother in peace. This is like a thief taking another thief to court, and suing him for making too much noise while he was robbing him, causing him to drop the television set that he was holding. This is the unpopular truth! So, in this equation, they are both wrong! So, when I tell Elizabeth the true cost of her freedom, chances are, she won't be willing to pay it. She'd look for someone else to ~~manipulate~~ counsel her mother. You see, they're both manipulative! Her mother's manipulative ways manifest through dominance, anger, control and maybe even through physical abuse. Elizabeth's manipulative ways manifest through her casting herself as the victim, not realizing that her ways are abusive as well. Again, she's connected to the right woman (her mother) in the wrong way!

Also, please note that there is no right way to connect to the wrong person. Consider this—I am a writer, graphic designer and photographer, just to name a few. If I applied to be a miner at a coal mine company, they'd reject my application. Why? Because I'm applying for a position that I'm not qualified for. But what if I told them the many trades, skills and talents that I have? Would that change their collective minds? No. Let's say that Elizabeth took my advice and moved out of her mother's house. She got a job, started going back to school and took full financial responsibility for herself. Does this mean that she can now have a healthy relationship with her mother? Absolutely not! Her mother will determine what roles she's willing to operate in, and what roles she has available in her life. So, if Elizabeth decides (which she should) that she will no longer tolerate mental, verbal, emotional or physical abuse from her mother or anyone for that matter, and if she aggressively and consistently enforces those boundaries, there's a big chance that her mother will exit her life. Sometimes, these dramatic exits are the narcissist's attempt to "punish" the empath, hoping that the empath will realize that he or she needs the narcissist and return to the role the narcissist has cut out for them. In other cases, the Jezebellic personality will decide that he or she doesn't want a relationship with his or her child simply because bound people hate boundaries. Either way, the Bible tells us that if the unbelieving wants to depart, let them depart. This isn't just referencing folks who don't believe in God, it's also referencing folks who don't believe in you! Some people will only tolerate you if you are willing to fit into one of the few toxic roles they've created for you; if you're not willing to accept any of these roles (which you shouldn't), they'll evict you from their lives or, at minimum, put you on punishment. Stop thinking that you can change these people! If you want a clear picture of what this looks like, imagine yourself sitting across the table from a person. That person slides a contract over to you, and the contract reads, "If you want to be a part of my life:

1. You have to let me control you.
2. You have to allow me to take out my anger on you, even if you're not the one who upset me.
3. You have to choose me over everyone and everything in your life, including your spouse and children.

4. You need to answer all of my calls, and you must do this on the first or second ring!
5. You have to accept full responsibility for my wrongs!
6. You have to defend me, even when I'm wrong—no, especially when I'm wrong!
7. You have to put me before God.
8. You have to pacify my rejection whenever it flares up.
9. You have to keep me occupied and entertained whenever I'm bored.
10. You have to let me abuse you in every way.
11. You don't get to prosper unless I prosper! And I'll determine how prosperous you should be!
12. You must be willing to risk it all for me.

Would you take a pen and sign this contract? Chances are, you wouldn't! But the majority of people who have soul-tied themselves to narcissists have pretty much signed this agreement, albeit, not physically. When this is the only role open in someone's life, you owe it to yourself to not apply for that role, continue in that role or allow yourself to be drafted into that role. It doesn't matter if they yell, cry, attack your character or if they just give you the silent treatment. However they manifest their demons, let them manifest; your job is to draw boundaries around yourself so they can't do this with your permission, whether that permission is communicated or through passive compliance. The point is, as you navigate through the many regions of thought, you will find yourself having to sever ties with some people, and either promote or demote others. The word "no" when used consistently and in the right context, will cause most of the people in your life to move to their rightful places, even if that means there is no place for them in your life. When I started drawing boundaries around myself, I was able to sort out the cords in my life. I was able to truly unplug from the people in my past by disconnecting from my past, forgiving those people and moving on to another region of thought. Yes, I experienced people walking out of my life who were dear to me, and I also experienced people taking lesser roles than the ones I'd voted them in or the roles they'd placed themselves in. I was in the hallway between two seasons, sorting out the cords attached to my soul. Was it painful? Yep! But more than that, it was worth it. I found peace when I disconnected from the wrong people and people whose presence in my life had expired. Again, they weren't always bad people. They were just in one region of thought while God was taking me to a new place. I had a choice. I could stay behind and learn to master those former regions of thought, and by doing this, I could stay connected to the people I'm most familiar with. I could grow old and boast about having been friends with those people for fifty-seven years. We could laugh and talk about all the crazy things we'd been through, and then, I could prematurely give up the ghost simply because there was no assignment for me in the season or region of thought that I'd committed myself to. Then, I could go before God and apologize for not having fulfilled my assignment on Earth, all because I chose my friends over my purpose.

—OR—

I could keep going if I only keep growing. We don't go forth, we grow forth. But if I keep moving forward, I'd lose some of the people and the things that were most dear to me. I'd be in God's will, so He'd do great and marvelous wonders through me, and I'd be able to help and impact the lives of far more people than I would have impacted had I stayed loyal to a season that was not loyal to me. Nevertheless, I'd have to count the cost and determine whether I'd be willing to pay the price for my "yes" to God's will. I'd have to be willing to go through the process of watching God unplug everything and everyone from my life, and then giving me the unpleasant task of untangling those connections. I'd have to make the difficult decision to not plug many of them back in. I'd have to deal with the accusations that come from the people I've outgrown, after all, I didn't leave them behind. I simply refused to stay behind and they refused to grow forth. Your family counted the cost, and many of your ancestors decided that they'd rather stay stuck and bound than to outgrow their connections. And it is for this reason that you've gone through much of what you went through as a child; it is for this reason that your family is in the condition it's in today. Don't keep falling down a bottomless pit, stuck in a cycle of defeat just to prove your loyalty to a bunch of broken people. Move on, growth forth and break out of all of the ungodly connections that you're in! When you break out of those connections, that's when you'll experience breakthrough!

Introducing Old Friends and Loved Ones to New Boundaries

Fear is one of Satan's favorite weapons. He readily uses it to keep us in check. And of course, one of those fears is the fear of losing the people we love, honor and respect the most. This is because we place value on our relationships, and over the course of this event we call life, we've all experienced what it is like to lose someone who we've held dear to our hearts. And I'm not talking about losing them to death, I'm talking about them walking away from us by choice. For many of us, it took some time for those wounds to heal. So, out of fear of experiencing that pain again, we often muzzle ourselves when we should be speaking up.

The million-dollar question for most people is, "How do I introduce the people in my life to my newfound boundaries? They're accustomed to me being one way, but how do I establish and enforce boundaries without offending them?" The short answer is, you can't. Offense is the language of the bound. The truth of the matter is, bound people hate boundaries; we've already established this. So, to get them to speak your language, you have to be willing to offend and potentially lose them. There are some people who simply will not be a part of your life <u>unless</u> you allow them to bind, blind and control you. I have these types of people in my family and they have absolutely nothing to do with me, and I'm okay with that. The reason I'm okay with it is this—I have two choices. I can either have them in my life, and allow them to control, manipulate and mismanage me or I can grieve those relationships and keep my peace. I obviously chose the latter. And I don't allow them to make me feel guilty for setting and enforcing boundaries at the expense of my relationship with them. Remember, setting boundaries is similar to creating a contract between yourself and another person. They get to pencil in what they require of you to have a relationship with them, and you get to pencil in what you require of them to have a relationship with you. If what they want requires you to be bound to your past, mistreated or manipulated, you shouldn't sign that contract. And by signing, I mean, you shouldn't keep these people around. Your job is to set some boundaries, and whenever or if ever they are to violate those boundaries, your job is to confront them and reinforce those boundaries. If they still refuse to honor them, you will have to make a difficult decision. What's in your best interest, of course, is to grieve those relationships and put space between yourself and those people. This doesn't mean that you have to entirely cut them out of your life (in some cases). Most times, you just have to demote them. In other words, you can't have the relationship you once had with them. A close family member would then become a distant family member. This means that you are not to share intimate details about your life with her, you would have to reduce the frequency of your communications with her and you'd have to tell her no more often. Let's say we're dealing with a narcissistic parent who absolutely refuses to treat you with love and respect. Let's say it's your mother. Every time she calls you, she's argumentative, condescending and/or manipulative. Call her out on it in the moment. Somehow, it has become culturally acceptable for people to have passive-aggressive conversations with one another. In other words, it's common for two people to sit on the phone and play mind games with one another. You shouldn't tolerate this behavior from anyone. Instead, if your mother is playing mind games, address it directly. Look at the dialogue below to get a better understanding. We'll create two characters—Jamie and her mother, Ms. Stokes.

Speaker	Wrong Way	Right Way
Jamie	Mom, I just ordered your Mother's Day gift. I'll bring it over to your house with me on Sunday.	Mom, I just ordered your Mother's Day gift. I'll bring it over to your house with me on Sunday.
Ms. Stokes	It's good to know that somebody is thinking about me. Maggie is always bragging about what her daughter got her. It'll sure be nice to shut her up for a change! Last year, her daughter bought her a Gucci bag, and she just could not stop	It's good to know that somebody is thinking about me. Maggie is always bragging about what her daughter got her. It'll sure be nice to shut her up for a change! Last year, her daughter bought her a Gucci bag, and

Speaker	Wrong Way	Right Way
	bragging about it. I can't wait to show her my gift.	she just could not stop bragging about it. I can't wait to show her my gift.
Jamie	Yeah, well, it's been hard for me ever since I got laid off from work, so while it's not a Gucci bag, I think it's pretty nice.	Yeah, well, it's been hard for me ever since I got laid off from work, so while it's not a Gucci bag, I think it's pretty nice.
Ms. Stokes	(Moment of silence). You know your sister is coming into town too. She said that she got me a gift as well. I know it's going to be big! She might be crazy, but she loves her mother.	(Moment of silence). You know your sister is coming into town too. She said that she got me a gift as well. I know it's going to be big! She might be crazy, but she loves her mother.
Jamie	Well, I love you too, you know. Anyway, what time does her flight touch down?	Mom, don't start with the mind games. I love you too, and you know this, but we're not about to have a toxic

Speaker	Wrong Way	Right Way
		conversation. I love you, I bought you a gift that I could afford, and I'll see you Sunday, so let's change the conversation or hang up.
Ms. Stokes	At noon on Saturday. She wanted to take me out shopping, so she's coming in a day early. You know Jason got a promotion on his job, so they're doing really good right now. He buys her whatever she wants. And he opted to stay home so she could spend the weekend with me. They don't make them like that anymore.	(Gasp) What are you talking about? See there, I wasn't trying to imply anything. I was just saying ....
Jamie	Well, you know that Tony loves you as well, and he's coming with me on Sunday.	Mom, if you and I are going to have a relationship, you are going to have to be

Speaker	Wrong Way	Right Way
	But Saturday, I'll try to swing through and say hi to Joyce before we head out. Me and Tony are traveling to Georgia on Saturday to see his mother. He wanted to give his mother her gift in person, and then, we're coming back Sunday so we can spend the day with you.	mindful of the words you say. Don't be passive-aggressive with me. Don't hint around or play mind games. I love you, but I'm not going to tolerate this. End of discussion. Now, I'll let you think about what I said and I'll see you on Saturday morning. Love you and talk to you later. Bye.
Ms. Stokes	No rush! I'm probably going to sleep in a little, so y'all get here whenever you can! I remember when Jason was all up under your sister, and wanted to go everywhere with her. She set that man straight! She trained him well!	

Speaker	Wrong Way	Right Way
Jamie	Well, Tony's not a Labrador Retriever, so I'm not going to train him, if that's what you're insinuating. Anyhow, I gotta go. I'll see you Saturday morning, Mom.	

In the dialogue labeled as "Wrong Way," Jamie spent too much time and energy having a play on words with her mother. She could clearly see where her mother was headed, but she did what most of us often do. She continued in the conversation, stopping to kindly address her mother's insinuations, instead of confronting them head on. Please know that it is not disrespectful to demand that others, including your parents, give you the same measure of respect that they demand from you. As you can see, Ms. Stokes was being manipulative in her words. It's painfully clear what she wants. She wants her daughter to:

1. Put herself in debt trying to compete with some woman named Maggie.
2. Compete with her sister. And she's using her love and affirmation as bait to achieve this.
3. Put her before her husband.

If this was my mother, I'd extract these three pointers from the conversation and point them out to her. I would then say, for example, "I'm not going to compete with Maggie's daughter. If you don't like the gift I give you, I'll take it back and save myself some money. I love my sister, and you are not going to make me compete with her for your attention. And last but not least, I am not going to train my husband. God is the head of Jesus, Jesus is the head of man, and man is the head of his wife. If you can't understand or honor this, we'll just stay at home." Now, in our culture, this is considered disrespectful, and that's why fifty percent of marriages end in divorce. This is why we have so many straitjacket qualified folks walking around. By me being upfront and confrontational about the issue, I am disallowing my mother from playing a bunch of mind games. In our culture, most people would just do a dance with their words, passively trying to correct their mothers without offending them. This is silly and it only causes the person defending themselves to become just as manipulative as their mothers. Offense is inevitable when you're setting and enforcing boundaries that bound people have to abide by. In other words, there's no getting around it! And please note that if Jamie did this the right way and she was consistent with enforcing her boundaries, her mother would either:

1. **Learn to respect her.** This can and does happen! Remember, this is similar to a contract. Jamie would have to let her mother know that there is one role open in her life, and that is for her to be a loving, respectful mother to her, mother-in-law to her husband and grandparent to her children. Her mother will decide whether she's willing to accept that

position or not. If not, Jamie would have to put space between her mother and her family.

2. **Walk out of her life.** This can and does happen as well! The truth is, there are some people who will not have anything to do with you unless they can manipulate and control you. You have to let them go, regardless of who they are and what role they serve in. Sometimes, after losing some of the people they love the most, they rethink their positions. They will then return and repent. If not, don't go chasing them, because by doing so, you are essentially agreeing to the terms listed in their contract for you.

3. **Give her daughter an ultimatum.** That is to accept her as she is or walk away. When this happens, you should always reject the contractual offer. Walk away. Some parents will use their children's love for them or dependency on them as a bargaining or bartering tool to get what they want. Disarm them by loving them from a distance and building your own wealth. Again, in some cases, they'll return and repent, oftentimes a year or more later after realizing that you are not going to give into their demands.

But when should you communicate your new boundaries to someone who's been a part of your life for a long time? Consider this—countries don't prepare for war in times of war, they prepare for war in times of peace. In other words, don't wait for your loved ones to do something offensive. You can address an issue once it arises, of course, but it is better to:

1. **Spell out your new boundaries.** Do this on paper so that you can see them.
2. **Communicate those boundaries.** For example, let's say that I decided that I will no longer allow my relatives to use profanity in my house because I'm Christian, plus, I don't want my children to be subjected to this. Let's say that my siblings liked to use profanity. I would wait until we had a conversation and tell them about my goals. I'd say, "So, I realized that I've been exposing my kids to some things they shouldn't be exposed to. I spoke with the kids and told them that using profanity is not okay. With that said, no more cursing around them. I've already told Dave about this and I wanted to make sure I tell you."
3. **Enforce those boundaries.** Going back to the aforementioned example, let's say that my sister either forgot about my new rules or decided to test them. One day, she's at my house and she starts cursing. I'd pull her aside and reinforce those rules. I'd say, for example, "What did I tell you? I asked you not to use profanity in front of my children. All I can do is ask you to respect my rules, ma'am. Please don't let me have to say this again."

Would my sister be offended? Yes! And I don't expect anything less! Especially since she would likely be accustomed to using profanity around my children. Anytime you establish and communicate new boundaries to the people in your life, you are pretty much introducing the new you to those people. I remember a former co-worker of mine loved to refer to her friends as female dogs. She and I were starting to take our lunch breaks together, so she was getting comfortable with me. One day, she shouted out, "What up, b*!@^?!" Immediately, I felt offended because she'd crossed a boundary, but I didn't address it on that day. She did this maybe three or four times before I decided to address it. I pulled her aside and told her to call me by my name. I was nice, but firm. I told her not to call me a b*!@^; I told her that I am a woman of God and that I only answered to my name. It became immediately obvious to me that no one had ever called her out on this before because she didn't know how to respond. Finally, she said, "Okay," before walking away. And for about two weeks, she would not speak to me at all. I knew that this was the risk I'd be taking by communicating my boundaries with her. But eventually, she started back speaking with me and we became really good friends. She wasn't a bad person. I just had to communicate my boundaries with her, otherwise, I would have run the risk of permanently losing her as a friend. The point is, communicating boundaries to people does make them feel a level of discomfort and offense. But you have to understand that you're not mismanaging or mistreating them by having those standards and enforcing them. All the same, you have to give them time to accept and adjust to your boundaries or decide if they want to be a part of your life.

Some boundaries are established as events take place. For

example, when I was in my late twenties, I told my siblings not to bring their insignificant others to my house. I told them that only fiances and spouses were allowed at my house. This was because I had a stepson I was raising, and I didn't want him to see them bringing new people to my house every other month. My mother and most of the women in my family had allowed our male relatives to do this, and consequently, many of the young boys in our families thought womanizing was okay. To date, I have told my family members who have live-in boyfriends and girlfriends that they could visit me (they live states away), but their boyfriends/girlfriends could not. If they came into town, they'd have to stay at a hotel. Of course, I've had relatives to suggest that I allow them to come down and sleep in separate rooms. That's a no-go for me! Because I know what they'd do the minute we all went to bed! They'd sneak around like school children. And these boundaries may seem unrealistic for many people because they've normalized sin and dysfunctional lifestyles. And get this—every home has an atmosphere. Most people, especially folks who are broken or rebellious, have a certain climate that they're most comfortable in. They bring these atmospheres with them wherever they go, so if you open your house to them, they will change the settings (rules) and set their own atmospheres in your house—if allowed! Consequently, their comfort would cost you your peace. And what's crazy is, because they fear confrontation, many people allow their homes to be overtaken every time their friends or family members pay them a visit! They reason within themselves that their visitors won't be there long, so their discomfort is temporary. No! Boundaries are designed to organize your relationships. Having no boundaries or seasonal boundaries equal disorder, and disorder equals dysfunction.

So, how do you introduce old friends and family members to new boundaries?

1. **Write them down somewhere.** You need to establish these new boundaries in your heart so that they won't end up being fluid boundaries. Remember, fluid boundaries are flexible, meaning, they are not solid. In other words, they can be moved or manipulated. To see a picture of this, get an empty water bottle and fill half of the bottle with small rocks. Fill the other half with water. Now, take your index finger and try to push the bottom of the bottle in. You'll find that you're able to push it a little bit, but not too much. This is because the rocks won't allow the bottle to be manipulated too much. Now, using that same index finger, push in the bottle more towards the top where you see water. You'll find this a lot easier to do. Even though the bottle has substance, one of those substances is not solid. This makes the bottle impressionable, pliant, modifiable or easy to be manipulated.

2. **Solidify your boundaries before you communicate them.** You do this by understanding why you need those boundaries in the first place. What are you trying to achieve? What would happen if you didn't establish those boundaries? In other words, count the

cost! Would you be willing to lose some relationships that are important to you by setting and establishing those boundaries? Consider the people in your life. How are they going to respond? Make sure you have an answer because some of them will question you.

3. **Get everyone in your house on board** if your new boundaries are for outsiders like family members or friends. If a bound person finds a weak spot in your home, he or she will utilize that person's weakness to get what he or she wants.

4. **Communicate your boundaries to the people in your life**, especially the folks who will be affected by them the most. Have that hard conversation with them that you've been trying to avoid. It'll be okay.

5. **Enforce your boundaries.** This is the hardest part of the process, but it's the most rewarding! This is oftentimes when you have to address the people who either violate your boundaries or try to get around them. For example, I often have potential clients who will email me what they want on a logo that they've seen on my site. I respond back with, "That's great! We're happy that you like the design! Once you purchase the design, we will gladly add your ministry's name to it. If you have any questions or you'd like to place your order over the phone, we will gladly assist you." This is nice enough and clear enough for anyone to understand, right? Howbeit, I still have people who respond with, "I can't pay for it until I see it." I'll typically respond back, letting them know that

we require one hundred percent of the design's cost upfront if it's in our store since it's already designed and they can clearly see it or, if they are ordering a custom design, we require fifty percent upfront. If they still offer some sort of rebuttal, I stop responding to them. And they will often go weeks or months without placing an order. This virtual stand-off is common for those of us who offer digital services. Nevertheless, many of them will reconnect with me once they've shopped around or finished throwing their tantrums. When they reach back out, I resend them the same message if they ask the same questions. Most of them will go ahead and place their orders, but a few will go find someone else to take advantage of. This is what enforcing boundaries look like! It looks like offended people, stand-offs, punishments and just about anything the human mind can conjure up. Nevertheless, it's all worth it in the end!

6. **Keep adding on to those boundaries!** When you first establish boundaries, you will notice that a lot of people in your life will look for and find what we call loopholes. These are the leaks in your system. You patch them up by adding new boundaries on top of the already established ones. For example, let's say that I said to my nephew, "You can't bring any of your girlfriends in my house." What I mean by this is, I don't want them to come to my place of residence because I don't want them to get mad at him one day and decide to bring their drama to my house.

Nevertheless, my nephew decides to be legalistic, so one day, I find him parked in front of my house with his girlfriend in his car. When I confront him, he says, "You said I couldn't bring a woman in your house. She didn't come in! We were outside the whole time." I would have to add on to my already established rules. So, I'd say, "You are not allowed to give my address to any of your girlfriends or invite them anywhere near my house." What I'm doing is securing my relationship with him. If I don't establish or enforce these boundaries, I'd likely become frustrated with him and I'd stop him from coming to my house altogether.

7. **Defend your boundaries.** This is inevitable. Some people are going to imply that your boundaries are unrealistic and maybe even over-the-top. This is because they can't bring their atmospheres with them to your house or establish their rules in your systems and processes. Do NOT rethink your boundaries unless they truly are unrealistic. And one way to see if they are unrealistic is by communicating them with someone who has achieved the results you want to achieve. Get their take on the matter.

8. **Reinforce your boundaries!** You've established them, you've added onto them and you've even enforced them, but any good set of boundaries has to absolutely be reinforced. This is your way of tightening the screws and covering any loose ends that may have developed over time or as a result of people pressing up against those boundaries.

Sometimes, you have to revisit your boundaries (this is why it's good to write them down) and re-communicate those boundaries to others. People will press up against them or try to wear them down.

9. **Respect your own boundaries!** I remember when the Lord gave me this command. I was allowing a few customers here and there to go around my already established rules simply because they were really nice or they wanted to place a large order. Of course, I didn't listen at first. I had to be disappointed and offended many times before I came to realize the power and the purpose of those boundaries. Again, people are going to try to get you to question your boundaries, relax your standards or remove those boundaries altogether. And they'll be able to successfully pull this off if you don't respect your own boundaries.

10. **Monitor your boundaries.** Discernment isn't just a feeling that comes over us when we look into the eyes of another human being. Discernment is more often the result of you watching and seeing how others respect your boundaries or the boundaries of others. When someone repeatedly violates your communicated and established boundaries, it's time for you to reposition that person in your life or out of your life. When Lot's herdsmen got into a spat with Abraham's herdsmen, he had to rethink Lot's position in his life. Abraham then sent Lot away in the kindest way. He said, "Let there be no strife between you and

me, and between your herdsmen and my herdsmen, for we are kinsmen. Is not the whole land before you? Separate yourself from me. If you take the left hand, then I will go to the right, or if you take the right hand, then I will go to the left." What we can take from this is, every separation isn't always contentious! Sometimes, you have to go back to the drawing board and revisit/rethink your relationship with people, and then, send them on their way.

Setting Boundaries in the Workplace

I'll say this. I genuinely, wholeheartedly and passionately believe that if we are to walk in our God-given authority, establishing and enforcing boundaries around ourselves, our families, our finances and everything that we consider sacred, we wouldn't lack for anything! We'd have the relationships we want, we'd have the money we want and we'd have the peace that surpasses all understanding. Our self-esteem would be at an all-time high, our confidence would begin to produce fruit and we'd find ourselves surrounded by people who genuinely and wholeheartedly want the best for us. But again, to get this, we have to count the cost and be willing to pay the price. And remember, the Big U or the big ultimatum. Anytime you establish and enforce boundaries, you will be put on punishment by some people. I often joke about having been placed on a lot of punishments, especially by immature believers. I think this is because many people don't know how to respond to boundaries and they don't realize that their behaviors are abusive and sometimes even demonic. Having survived many years of abuse, I can easily recognize these behaviors and call them out. When communicating with people who exhibit these traits, I often emphasize the power and the purpose of communication. For example, I'll say, "Refusing to speak to me isn't going to force me to do what you want me to do. It only shows me your character." I also tell them that this behavior is low-level abuse. If they continue in it, they'll become more and more abusive until they find themselves surrounded by folks who tolerate them. To be abusive doesn't necessarily mean that you are verbally, mentally or physically attacking someone. One narcissistic trait is ignoring a person when that person does not give you what you want or do whatever it is you want them to do. Anyone who's been raised by a narcissist is familiar with this wile. It's designed to make you insecure, invoke fear in your heart and get you to give into that person's demands. And sometimes, the person hasn't made an open request. Sometimes, we offend people by not doing things that they assumed we should automatically know to do. Life and experience have taught me that people like that don't make good friends; they are often entitled, competitive and manipulative. In other words, they have mastered a region of thought and they've learned to master people in that region of thought by putting them in a time-out of sorts. And it goes without saying that you have to keep people like that at arm's length away from you. And of course, someone's going to ask, "What if I have no choice but to deal with that person? What if I work with a person like that?" I've worked with people like this, and I've worked with them in close proximity. In some cases, I've just let them be because I wasn't there to make friends, but if it started affecting my ability to perform my job, I would:

1. **Go home and sort the issue out.** I NEVER confront a person without me first analyzing the situation. The

reason is because emotional conversations typically end badly, but logical ones are oftentimes efficient and productive. So, I look at the situation, not just from a personal point of view, but from an objective point of view. I consider what I may have potentially done or said to offend the person, and then, I put myself in that person's shoes. What would I have done? I consider my interactions with that person, my body language and my tone. I consider every reason the person may have an issue with me, and I look for evidence to support my theory. This way, I can properly address the matter, so we don't end up having a passive-aggressive play on words. I like to call an issue out head-on, not so I can appear smart, but so we can get to the bottom of it. Be sure to get to the root of the matter and find where you're wrong; this way, you can apologize for anything you've said that may have been offensive, anything you've done that may have been offensive and any misconceptions that may have arisen. Sorting your issues out from theirs will keep you from blaming the person for your own insecurities and wrongs. You want that individual to listen and not see the conversation as an argument or a dual of sorts. You want him or her to see it as you caring enough to address the matter.

2. **Go to the manager and voice my concerns**, letting the manager know that I plan to pull the person aside and speak with them about the issue. This allows the

manager to weigh in and, for example, say, "I want to be in that meeting" or the manager would give me some tips. This also protects me from being disciplined should the person get offended whenever I address him or her.

3. **Set up a meeting with that person.** For example, I would say, "Good morning, Elma. You're just the person I want to see. I hope your day is off to a great start. Anyhow, the reason I stopped you is because I want to possibly set up a meeting with you today around lunch time. There are some things I'd like to discuss with you. Are you available to speak today for around fifteen to thirty minutes?" Chances are, Elma will agree to the meeting, but if she gives me the runaround, I'll set it up for the next day. If she continues to give me the runaround, I'd have our boss to set up a meeting with all three of us. If she asks, "What about?" I wouldn't go into details right there in the moment because it's out in the open. This could lead her to feel the need to defend herself. I would just say, "Some workplace issues that I've been having. Nothing too bad. I'd rather discuss it when we have about fifteen to thirty minutes to sit down, away from everyone." What I'm doing is insisting on having an orderly meeting in a controlled environment; this way, I can avoid having an emotional meeting where she feels the need to defend herself rather than just listen to what I'm saying.

4. **Communicate my issue with the person** and

assume responsibility for my role in the miscommunication! It is human nature to go on the defensive, especially when confronted by people you don't have a relationship with or you have a negative history with. The first few minutes of these types of meetings are typically about dismantling and disallowing any misconceptions or preconceptions to form. I'd start off by telling Elma what I admire about her, but I wouldn't spend too much time beating around the bush. Instead, I'd say something to the effect of, "Hey Elma, you look amazing today, as always! You have to tell me where you got those shoes!" After a few seconds or minutes of small talk, I'd say, "Well, the reason I asked to meet with you is because I wanted to personally apologize to you because I feel like we've gotten off to a bad start, and I know that I can sometimes be stand-offish." From here, I'd list what I discovered during the sorting process, and then, I'd apologize for anything I may have done or said. After that, I'd continue with, "I've also noticed that you don't speak to me, and anytime I make a mistake or you think I've made a mistake, your tone towards me is very condescending. I don't want to have a contentious relationship with any of my colleagues. While we may not necessarily be friends, we don't have to be enemies. So, if I do something wrong, I appreciate your healthy feedback, and I wanted to make sure that you're comfortable coming to me in a professional manner. I admire you and I want to have a good working relationship with you, but you raising your voice or being condescending towards me is not something I can accept. I wanted to address this so that you could hear my heart and know that you can come to me if there is an issue, but just do it in a professional manner. So, if there's anything I've done wrong or said that may have offended you, I apologize for it right now and I ask for your forgiveness. If it's something I repeatedly do, let me know so I can make the necessary adjustments. But from here on out, I don't want to ever have another argument with you, after all, we work together. We're here to help this company to become a success, and we can't do that if we're contending or competing with one another."

5. **Be accountable.** I'd make sure I let the manager know that I had the meeting with Elma, and I'd tell her (or him) how it went. If we're dealing with someone outside the workplace, I'd let my mentor know how that meeting went.

And remember, established boundaries not only have to be enforced, they have to be reinforced from time-to-time. You may have to pull the person aside again and remind him or her of your boundaries. If the behavior is not curved, chances are, you will have to get a mediator involved. For example, you may have to involve your manager. However you do it, make sure you get to the root of the issue and ALWAYS follow protocol! This is your safe place. A lot of times, people who've mastered a region of thought will begin to play mind games; they'll start talking about everything but the issue at hand because they're too embarrassed to say, for example, "I don't like how fast you're ascending in this corporation" or "You think you're better than me." So, they'll try to talk about everything underneath the sun, except the problem at hand. When this happens, address what you see. For example, I would say to Elma, "No, I noticed a shift in your behavior towards me when Mrs. Manning acknowledged me at a meeting and said that I was doing a great job. And I want you to know that I am no threat to your position. I'm just trying to do my best to be an asset wherever I go." When you confront an issue like this head-on—when you call a demon by its name, you can rest assured that the person will respond negatively; he or she is not going to be honest. For example, Elma would never say, "Yes, I feel threatened by you, so I am doing everything in my power to sabotage you! I want you to lose your job! Everyone who's gotten any measure of success in this company has always gone through me! They had to win favor with me first; this way, I felt assured that they wouldn't be a threat to my position, plus, this allowed me to take some measure of credit for their success! But you didn't do that! You didn't kiss up behind me or try to win favor with me, and I didn't consider you a real threat until Mrs. Manning brought your name up in a meeting! Do you know that I couldn't get you off my mind that entire day?! How dare you be great outside of my influence! This is why I am condescending towards you! This is why I manipulated everyone else into not speaking to you. I led the charge, and since they still think they need me to succeed, they saw how I treated you and followed suit! They are followers, and this is what I appreciate about them, but you have the audacity to act like a leader! No one succeeds in this organization without my permission!" Do you see how immature, unreasonable and narcissistic this rant is? Now, you can understand why she would NEVER tell you the truth. She'd find something that you actually did wrong (minor or major) and point it out. This is why I like to study people from afar. So, if they point out something I did wrong, I point out similar wrongs in the people they seem to favor. In other words, I dismantle their lies until nothing but the truth stands.

But what if the person who's coming against you in the workplace is your manager? What should you do then? It's simple—follow protocol. Whenever you honor the rules and systems of an organization, you make it difficult for people to effectively sabotage you. I've witnessed people going up against folks who were mishandling them, only for them (the victims) to be terminated and demonized. This was because they were emotional; they were too quick to open their mouths when the Bible tells us to be slow to speak and slow to anger (see James 1:19). The crazy part is that they were right—they pointed out the repeated injustices and schisms that were at play, but they did this in the wrong manner. They got upset one day and decided to confront their workplace oppressors. Consequently, the oppressors ended up getting the best of them because they were able to remain logical while the other person was emotional. The oppressors were able to say, for example, "I don't know what you're talking about," and these words often were enough to trigger the person who'd been victimized. They'd return with, "You do know what I'm talking about!" And they'd follow those words with facts, but again, they did this in the wrong way. The oppressor was able to use those moments to deflect all of the wrongdoing onto the victim because in those moments, the victim looked and sounded like the oppressor, and the oppressor looked and sounded like a victim. So, they end up losing their jobs and being filled with hatred towards their former oppressors. Managers and supervisors may have more power in an organization, but this doesn't mean that they are untouchable. If you follow the systems and protocols established in that organization, you'll increase the likelihood of you having longevity within that company. So, if you're having trouble with your manager or a supervisor, be sure to follow the steps above. Be sure to contact the manager's manager before you say something to the manger; this way, you can lessen the chances of workplace retaliation.

Remember, you should establish boundaries around everything that you want to keep and anything that you want to contain or limit. If you want to keep your job and prosper in your workplace, it is essential that you establish and enforce some boundaries there, but make sure they are realistic. And most importantly, set boundaries around your heart so that what you experience in the workplace won't negatively impact you. And remember, the job you have may be a launching pad that God is using to propel you to your next level. Be sure to manage your emotions well, treat everyone with love and respect, and always make it a point to be an asset and not a liability.

SETTING BOUNDARIES IN RELATIONSHIPS

The Bible says, "Rebellion is as the sin of witchcraft," but the world says, "Rules are meant to be broken." As a matter of fact, the rebel is considered a hot commodity in the world AND in some churches today. The more rebellious a man is, the more some women find him attractive. All the same, many immature and rebellious believers are still attracted to bound people. It's not uncommon to hear a believing woman say that she wants her husband to have the best of both worlds; she wants him to be saved and filled with the Holy Ghost, BUT she also wants him to "have them hands." This is slang for, not just being <u>able</u> to physically fight, but being <u>ready</u> to physically fight should the occasion call for it. And to be honest, we all want someone who can defend us, but that's not the issue. The problem is in the "type" of guy they feel most secure with. It's typically the struggling thug or rebel who's bound by pride, doesn't follow the rules, will not submit to God, will not submit to any other authority, but has a hint of Christianity about him. In other words, these women are attracted to the Leviathan spirit. Of course, most women who reason like this are still babes in Christ, even though they are sometimes skilled at doing church. They know scriptures and they know how to pray, but something in them still wants a man who's caught between two systems. They want the man who looks both ways before entering the land of Sin to get the blackberries, the raspberries, the strawberries and the blueberries, just as long as he makes it back through the window before it closes and just as long as he doesn't touch another woman while he's over there. They love looking into the eyes of a rejected and broken soul. They love the calloused hands of rebellion, the stiff neck of pride and the soft porn that society calls pillow talk.

Thankfully, some of these women will eventually mature and find themselves wanting a more stable and mature man of God. This normally happens after they get the man that they want, only to have him repeatedly disappoint them. After they see some masculine, God-fearing men covering their wives in prayer, casting out demons and leading the charge in their households, most women normally have a change of heart. This typically happens when their marriages or relationships begin to break down because they then start comparing their husbands to the men they once rejected. Then again, there are many of them who will commit themselves to a man while in the wrong regions of thought. They won't just commit to the man, but they'll commit to the mindset that led them to the man. The same is true for many believing men. They are attracted to the double-minded, seductive women who they see at church every other Sunday. But unlike women, most of them are not looking to commit to their partners. They want prideful, confident, but insecure women who know how to wear their pain well; this is because they want the benefits of marriage without the responsibilities that come with being a husband. Consequently, many of them will never reach their full potential in the realm of the Earth. This is why God told us to seek first the Kingdom of God and all His righteousness, and by doing so, He said that everything else will be added to us. But when we're immature, we often try to silence our voids (lack of information, abundance of unprocessed trauma) by using people as bandages.

Do you remember the clown we discussed earlier? In the aforementioned analogy, we discussed a little girl being told by her parents at her third birthday party that she had to pick a husband for herself from her guests. This would be the guy that she'd marry when she turned 18. Because she was young and immature, she quite naturally picked the clown who had been hired to entertain her. But eventually, she got older, and when the time came for her to commit to the choice she'd made while still a toddler, she wasn't happy about it. While this is just an analogy, it is a clear picture of what many men and women are faced with today. The choices that we make when we are babes in Christ or, better yet, in our seasons of immaturity, oftentimes become the storms of tomorrow. In truth, our courtrooms are filled with men and women who are trying to untangle themselves from the commitments they made when they didn't yet have a sober mind. Sadly enough, many of them are so wounded by those choices that they never escape the regions of thought they're in. They get divorced and remarried while still in the same mindset. And if you were to ask them about their failed relationships, because of their immaturity, they will shift the blame to their exes, rather than taking accountability for their own mistakes. Consequently, they suffer through many failed relationships. Galatians 4:1-5 speaks to this; it reads, "Now I say, That the heir, as long as he is a child, differeth nothing from a servant, though he be lord of all; but is under tutors and governors until the time appointed of the father. Even so we, when we were children, were in bondage under the elements of the world." Let's extract a few notes from this scripture:

1. The aforementioned individual is an heir; this means that he or she has an inheritance.
2. While the heir is still a child, he is no different than a servant or, better yet, a slave. Child, in this context, means immature. While we are still immature, we think, reason and behave as bound or unsaved people. And the word "child" is referring to a season or a stage of development.
3. The heir is lord of all. In other words, he not only has an inheritance, but he also has a measure of legal authority, howbeit, he cannot and will not tap into this authority until he has matured. Immature people who have been granted any measure of authority oftentimes abuse their power and the people under them.
4. He is under tutors and governors. These are the mentors and the leaders that God will use to shift our thinking. These are also the books, the videos and all of the lessons we'll learn in passing. Any person who refuses to be intentionally and consistently discipled by another person is someone who has chosen his

comfort over his inheritance.

5. ...until the time appointed of the Father. This scripture isn't dealing so much with time as we know it, but it deals with seasons or regions of thought. This is why God said for us to seek first the Kingdom of God and all His righteousness AND THEN all these things would be added to us. The reason this is important to note is because a lot of Christians are sitting around, waiting on their blessings and their deliverance to break into their homes or their churches and overtake them. Meanwhile, their blessings and their deliverance are aimlessly waiting for them in their next season.

6. When we were children, we were in bondage under the elements of the world. In other words, when we are immature, we are CARNAL! Carnal people are in bondage to the elements (riches, influence, power) of this world! They genuinely believe that if they were to get everything they want, that they'd be happy and all of their problems would go away. This is the evidence of their immaturity! Wealth doesn't slay demons; it only attracts more of them!

7. But when the fullness of time came... Again, this isn't dealing with time as we know it, it's dealing with the completion of a season! When the heir is no longer a child; in other words, when the heir no longer thinks or reasons irresponsibly, he can then receive his inheritance! Apostle Paul said it this way, "When I was a child, I spake as a child, I understood as a child, I

thought as a child: but when I became a man, I put away childish things" (1 Corinthians 13:11).

There's a season for everything! Ecclesiastes 3:1-8 says, "To everything there is a season, and a time to every purpose under the heaven: A time to be born, and a time to die; a time to plant, and a time to pluck up that which is planted; a time to kill, and a time to heal; a time to break down, and a time to build up; a time to weep, and a time to laugh; a time to mourn, and a time to dance; a time to cast away stones, and a time to gather stones together; a time to embrace, and a time to refrain from embracing; a time to get, and a time to lose; a time to keep, and a time to cast away; a time to rend, and a time to sew; a time to keep silence, and a time to speak; a time to love, and a time to hate; a time of war, and a time of peace." There is a season for you to be in a relationship, but first, there are several seasons that you shouldn't be dating anyone. This doesn't make you a bad person; it simply means that you're not mature enough to understand the complexity of love and long-suffering. You're still under tutors and governors or, at least, you should be. This is not an offensive statement; it simply means that you're not ready yet. Think of it this way—a millionaire dies and leaves his fortune to his only surviving child—a 15-year old boy by the name of Samson. Do you see where I'm going with this? He may as well have left his fortune to Delilah because that's who's going to get it if some other immoral woman doesn't beat her to it. But let's say that this particular Samson was born in the 21st century and he wasn't so into girls just yet. Instead, his vice is video games. By the time he turns 18, he'd be broke. This is because he's immature, and immature people are emotional. Everything they do is centered around their feelings, including shopping. A teenage boy is the perfect example of flesh in the hallway of a season. He's in the wilderness between childhood and adulthood. Again, this is why God wants us to seek Him first, and not just the Kingdom of God, but also, all His righteousness. In other words, study and show yourself approved; go and grow your faith. Your faith in God is your trust in God. People who can admit that they are not ready for a relationship are the ones who intentionally get ready. Everyone else just tells themselves that they are ready because they're adults, and based on their own standards, they are good people. It's great for you to examine yourself, but you also need someone who's not afraid to lose you to examine you. I'm talking about a leader or a mentor, and this, of course, has to be someone who's not romantically interested in you and someone you're not romantically interested in. I say this because there are some people who actually choose their mentors and their pastors because they are romantically, not spiritually, attracted to them. They then begin to adjust their personalities to fit the mentor or the leader's personality so that they can win the attention or favor of these people. They study these people from afar and adjust everything about themselves from their dress codes, their doctrinal beliefs to their diets, to accomplish their agenda, which normally is to foster an illegal relationship with the people in their sight. This chameleon-like spirit is called the Delilah spirit. Again, you need someone who's God-fearing and Holy Spirit filled to lead and/or mentor you. And they need time to get to know you so that they can tell you whether or not they believe you are ready for a relationship. All the same, you have to trust and honor them enough to take them at their words. I've told some of my mentees and former mentees that they weren't ready. Some people trusted me enough to go and get ready; others went looking for someone to tell them otherwise, and guess what? They found these people! This is why the Bible says that there is safety in the multitude of counsel. And because they didn't want to wait until God led them to the season of courtship, they were like the three-year old who chose a clown to be her future husband. It goes without saying that they ended up getting their hearts broken a few times and still having to wait! Howbeit, they had to heal as they waited, and the ones who refused to heal delayed their next seasons all the more! They were like those children in the backseat of their parent's car, repeatedly asking, "Are we there yet?" Again, there is a season for everything.

But first, what are some of the signs that you are mature enough to court?

1. **God is first and foremost in your life.** I'm not talking about claiming that He's first; He has to be the head of all of your decisions. If He's truly first in your life, chances are, He's the first someone you speak to when you wake up, you consult Him before making any major decisions, you honor the leaders He's put

in place, etc.

2. **You hate sin.** People who are lackadaisical in regards to sin are the ones who love it, and by sin, I'm not talking about the works of the flesh, I'm talking about the heart of distrust which leads to the works of the flesh. Mature people are not just compliant with God's will, they are passionate about it. And this passion is not based on religion, it's based on their intimate knowledge of God.

3. **You have standards that you've established AND enforced** with your family and friends. For example, they know that they can't bring their insignificant others to your house and have sex, they can't curse around you, and if they don't share the same faith as you, they cannot dishonor your faith, especially in your presence. This isn't a popular pointer nowadays because people have itching ears, and itching ears are what we refer to in the business world as a demand or a commodity. Wherever there's a demand, there will be someone willing to meet that demand—if the price is right.

4. **Your altar is bloody.** Your altar is your personal place of sacrifice. What have you given up for God's glory? This isn't to say that you need to be looking around, trying to figure out what you can give up; instead, what has God asked you to give up? Your level of sacrifice should match your level of calling. Abraham had to give up the close relationship he had with his nephew (Lot), he had to sacrifice animals and he had

to sacrifice his relationship as he knew it with his son, Ishmael. Moses had to sacrifice his comfort and all the trappings of success that he'd been raised with. And if you need some New Testament examples, look at Apostle Paul. He sacrificed his former religious beliefs and a high-ranking position as a Pharisee to preach the gospel. Apostle Stephen and many of the apostles of that era sacrificed their lives. Of course, Jesus sacrificed His life. Nowadays, God often requires us to sacrifice mindsets or, better yet, regions of thought, and while this sounds easy enough, there are some relationships and opportunities that will fall away or be snatched from us the moment we exit these regions of thought. So, the sacrifice is changing your mind at the detriment of those relationships and doors. And by "require," I don't mean that this is mandated of you to go to Heaven (Jesus paid the price for your soul); it simply means that before you can walk into your next season, you have to be willing to walk out of your current season. How many seasons are behind you, or are you still in the same place that you were in three years ago?

5. **You are prudent.** Another word for "prudent" is "sober." In other words, you take careful consideration of the choices you make today because your future does matter to you. You're not mainly led by your emotions or your needs; instead, you will sacrifice your desires for the greater good of your future and those around you. Prudence shows up in how we

212

shop, what we eat and what we take in intellectually. A prudent man or woman, for example, will get counseling if he or she needs it. A prideful person, on the other hand, won't.

6. **You understand and respect your single season.** This is important because many believers treat their single seasons like it's a disease and a curse. Remember, a season is nothing but a mindset! People who hate the seasons they're in miss the point of those seasons. In other words, they don't try to study and show themselves approved for the next season; instead, they invest that time and energy into decorating themselves like a bunch of Christmas trees, hoping that someone will pass by and pick them from the lineup. People who respect their single season, on the other hand, utilize that time and grace to learn, to get some deliverance, to get counseling (if needed), to build (books, businesses, etc.) and to cultivate.

7. **You've taken sex off the menu!** Here's what I learned—fornication, premarital sex or however you choose to refer to it is a heart condition. It's not just an act; it's a fruit, and every fruit has (1) ground, (2) roots and (3) something or someone watering it. The ground of a belief is the system backing that belief. God doesn't back sexual immorality; He's against it! We all know this, but a double-minded man or woman usually goes between two systems—the Kingdom of God and the systems of this world. Immature people

are double-minded until they mature; that's a given—we've all been there at some point! The roots represent the mind of a person. Remember, another word for "mindset" is region of thought. And lastly, the thing or the person watering that mindset is you and the people you surround yourself with. If you intend to grow, you need people around you who aren't afraid to lose you. My pastor refers to them as cutters. If you surround yourself with enablers (people who make you feel better about being out of God's will), you will find yourself stuck in a cycle of defeat! You'd be anointed, appointed, filled with the Holy Spirit and STUCK! Sure, if you fall into sexual immorality, your friends shouldn't beat you up, but they should've told you not to be alone with your insignificant other in the first place! They should hold you to a standard! People who are assigned to your future actually care about your future.

8. **You are financially independent** or heading in that direction. In all truth, this is an example of prudence. And of course, this doesn't mean that you need to be independently wealthy; what it means is that you shouldn't be relying on anyone but God to meet your needs or, at least, building in that direction (going to college, learning a trade, etc.). Needy people often choose their mates based on their needs and their fears. Their prayers for spouses are often driven by their needs; this causes them to be impatient with God, and it often drives them to sin against God. Of

course, someone who is dependent on others AND isn't doing anything to change this is in a region of thought. In other words, that person is immature. However, someone who is dependent on others, BUT is doing something to change this is a person who is mature enough to know that he or she needs to mature. Let that sink in. That person is in the hallway of two seasons, meaning, he or she is making progress!

9. **You are independent of man's influence.** In other words, you're not under the bondage of anyone's opinion! This one is a difficult one to layout because there are so many layers to it! On one hand, there are some people whose opinions you should care about because they are assigned to you in one way or another. This doesn't mean that you have to hide who you are, but it does mean that you have to be willing to adjust what you've become because of what you've gone through. In other words, they have to be able to correct and challenge you. And please don't mistake this to mean that you don't need a pastor, a mentor or someone to influence you because YOU DO! However, what this means is that you're not under the bondage of public opinion. By public, I mean that you aren't distracted, moved or inspired by people who have no stock in your life.

10. **You have forgiven the people who've hurt, rejected and abandoned you!** This is important because to be in unforgiveness means that you are

still in the season that you got hurt in. One way to forgive people is to take accountability for your own wrongs, even if the only thing you did wrong was giving your time and energy to those people. It means that you didn't test the spirit. When you take accountability for your own mistakes, you are less likely to repeat those mistakes.

But let's say that you have matured or, at least, you think you're mature enough for a relationship. How do you draw boundaries in relationships to ensure that you don't end up bound? How do you ensure that you don't end up soul-tied to the weapon that was formed against you? It's simple. Obey the Word of God. The Word is a boundary designed to keep the wrong people out of your life, but you have to stay within God's will if you want to reap the benefits of it. And to stay within God's will, you have to familiarize yourself with His Word. Next, you must identify your strengths and weaknesses. For example, I took kissing off the menu because it's pointless in a non-marital relationship. It only serves to connect us emotionally when, in truth, we need to get to know one another both logically and spiritually; this is what leads to a strong emotional connection later on. The logic behind this is—why heat up the oven if you're not planning to put anything in it? I have absolutely no plans to go back into sexual immorality. I am wholeheartedly against it now. So, why would I tempt myself and another human being? So, I drew a barrier around my lips; one that will only be lifted by the pastor who officiates my wedding when he or she says, "You may now kiss the bride." Again, the Word of God is a barrier designed to keep the enemy out. For example, I've been living in my current house for four years now, and I've had the same issue every year. During the winter, I'll normally start seeing millipedes in my house, and during the summer, I'll normally start seeing pill bugs in my house. Now, mind you, I live in Georgia so I'm guessing this isn't completely too abnormal. To remedy this, I purchased a chemical called Home Stop Bug Barrier. Every year, I have to create a barrier around my house with this chemical; I have to do this at least twice a year. When I start seeing pill bugs, I'll take thirty minutes of my time to go around the outside of my house with the spray. When I see millipedes, I do the same. This normally remedies the problem and I'm able to go back to my usual day-to-day. Millipedes and pillbugs (also known as roly pollies) are pests. In other words, they are not welcome. Now, imagine that I saw this problem, complained about it constantly, but did nothing about it. To make matters worse, I called you every single day, complaining about a bunch of bugs invading my home. It would be clear that I just want your attention, right? Because this is a problem that somebody else already created a solution for. In other words, I don't have to deal with it if I don't want to. This is what a lot of people do; they keep attracting a specific type of person, and then, complaining without getting to the source of the problem. And with these people, you have to draw a boundary around your ears since they won't draw one around their hearts. All the same, the solutions to their issues are readily available in the form of pastors, mentors, books, webinars and of course, the Bible! So, people don't have to sit in a toxic region of thought if they don't want to. However, they will have to invest time, effort and energy into getting the information they need to make a change.

Setting boundaries in relationships is something you should do before you enter a relationship, after all, countries don't prepare for war in times of war, they prepare for war in times of peace. All the same, your local grocery store doesn't order supplies after you walk in needing them. They stay in business by making sure they order what you and others need in advance. The Bible calls this being prudent! Proverbs 19:14 says, "House and riches are the inheritance of fathers: and a prudent wife is from the LORD." In other words, it is wise for you to prepare yourself in advance, otherwise, you'll be led by your emotions and your needs. An emotional spouse is a foolish one. All the same, foolish people tend to attract foolish people. How do you set boundaries in relationships? First, let's discuss how you should prepare yourself BEFORE you even consider dating or courting anyone. Look at the tips below.

#	Tips	Scriptural Backing
1	**Mature!** Get to know God first, and then, get to know yourself before	**Galatians 4:1-3** Now I say, That the heir, as long as he is a child, differs nothing from a servant, though he be lord of all; but is under tutors and governors until

#	Tips	Scriptural Backing
	you get into a relationship with anyone else. You do this by studying the Word of God, getting into a stable church home and submitting to Godly headship.	the time appointed of the father. Even so we, when we were children, were in bondage under the elements of the world.
2	**Get free!** Please note that freedom is a product of knowledge; it's more than an emotional experience that you have at church. Getting set free from demons is great, but you still need to dismantle demonic systems and replace them with Godly	**Matthew 7:3-5** And why beholdest thou the mote that is in thy brother's eye, but considerest not the beam that is in thine own eye? Or how wilt thou say to thy brother, Let me pull out the mote out of thine eye; and, behold, a beam *is* in thine own eye? Thou hypocrite, first cast out the beam out of thine own eye; and then shalt thou see clearly to cast out the mote out of thy brother's eye.

#	Tips	Scriptural Backing
	systems. This is because you won't set stable or realistic boundaries if you're bound. All the same, marriage is about helping one another. This is why the Bible refers to wives as help meets. But how can you help someone if you can't help yourself?	
3	**Govern yourself!** You need to master self-governance before you start noticing or reaching for the specks in other folks' eyes.	**Proverbs 25:28** He that hath no rule over his own spirit is like a city that is broken down, and without walls.

#	Tips	Scriptural Backing
4	**Present your laws and watch the people scatter.** That's what rules are designed to do; they are created to chase away the lawless. Another word for lawless is rebellious. Anyone who rebels against God with you will rebel against you. If you don't believe this, just keep on living.	**1 Timothy 8:1-11** But we know that the law is good, if a man use it lawfully; knowing this, that the law is not made for a righteous man, but for the lawless and disobedient, for the ungodly and for sinners, for unholy and profane, for murderers of fathers and murderers of mothers, for manslayers, for whoremongers, for them that defile themselves with mankind, for menstealers, for liars, for perjured persons, and if there be any other thing that is contrary to sound doctrine; according to the glorious gospel of the blessed God, which was committed to my trust.
5	**Keep growing!** In other words, keep studying the Word of God, disciplining yourself in every area, taking accountability for your mistakes,	**Hebrews 6:1** Therefore leaving the principles of the doctrine of Christ, let us go on unto perfection; not laying again the foundation of repentance from dead works, and of faith toward God.

#	Tips	Scriptural Backing
	learning from those mistakes, seeking the heart and the face of God and keep forgiving people along the way!	

All the same, two of the most important tools that you can have are:

1. **A made-up mind.** You get this by studying the Word until you agree with the Word. For example, I solidified my decision to do things God's way nearly a decade ago, and I didn't make this decision as a single woman. I made this decision while I was in the midst of a troubled marriage. I'd studied, prayed and died my way out of a bunch of self-inflicted and generational strongholds, realized the error of my ways, took accountability for my wrongs, repented, and then, said to God (and myself), "If I'm ever single again, I will never go back into fornication. Ever! I will never unequally yoke myself to an unbeliever—ever!" Get this—studying and spending time with God woke me up and sobered me up! And because my mind is made up, I now value my own time! In other words, I don't entertain time-wasters. A made-up mind is a powerful weapon against the enemy.

2. **A content heart.** Anyone who is not content will be

contentious. You have to be content as an individual, otherwise, you won't be content as a unit.

But what if you're already in a relationship? How do you hit reset and establish boundaries that are Godly, realistic and effective?

1. **Create boundaries for yourself first and master enforcing them!** One of the greatest and most effective weapons AGAINST a relationship is hypocrisy! It's not uncommon to come across individuals who set boundaries for their significant and insignificant others, but will not comply with those same boundaries. This is the quickest way to lose the respect of the person you're dating, courting or married to. For example, if you're not comfortable with your girlfriend, boyfriend or spouse hanging out with people of the opposite sex, you have to lead by example!

2. **Make sure your boundaries are realistic!** Don't set silly boundaries that are nearly impossible to comply with.

3. **Set boundaries together!** Don't just show up at a meeting with a bunch of rules. The only set rules you should bring with you are the ones set by God. But the two of you should sit down and discuss every other concern that you have or boundaries that you think should be implemented.

4. **Never agree with a boundary that you can't live with.** Everyone is different; not all couples have the

same rules, and what works for one couple may not work for you. One of the reasons you have to set boundaries is so you can determine whether the person you're dating or courting is compatible with you. This is why both of you should remain logical; another phrase for "logical" is sober-minded. This way, you can honestly communicate who you are, what you want, what you don't want, and your insignificant other can do the same.

5. **Compromise.** Of course, make sure you honor the Word of God and abide by it; that's a boundary that cannot be compromised! However, some boundaries should be communicated, considered and then the two of you can reach a compromise, just as long as it doesn't go against the Word of God. Boundaries that you should not compromise are the ones that put you one step closer to sexual immorality. For example, if you know you can't handle kissing without getting aroused, take it off the menu and add it to your non-negotiable list. All the same, you shouldn't allow your insignificant other in your home or vice versa; the two of you should not be left alone in a private setting. This is to lessen the chance that you'll fall into sexual immorality.

6. **Don't force a boundary on a person who doesn't want to abide by it.** For example, if I met a guy and told him about my no-kiss policy, he has the right to contest it. Now, because it's one of my non-negotiable or solid boundaries, I'm not going to relax or remove

that boundary. However, if this is something he's passionate about, and if he absolutely feels like he HAS to kiss his girl before they get married, I wouldn't force my beliefs on him, just like I wouldn't allow him to force his lips on me. We'd likely come to a mutual understanding that we are incompatible, and while this may seem outlandish and extreme to some, every person knows what they NEED to refrain from. If this is something he's insistent about, chances are, he's not against sex before marriage; he may know it's wrong, but he's not entirely against it. If I compromised and kissed him, you can rest assured that this wouldn't be the only boundary he'd come up against. Before long, he'd be complaining about not being able to be alone with me, and if I compromised on that, he'd complain about not being able to go into my bedroom, and if I compromised on that, he'd complain about me refusing to spoon with him. In other words, he would be advancing towards what he wants, which goes completely against my beliefs and my standards. Remember, boundaries are designed to CHASE AWAY bound people, and they only work if you employ them.

7. **Don't let someone outside of your relationship make you feel bad about your boundaries!** Let's say that you're out on a lunch date with your insignificant other (this is just my way of saying boyfriend or girlfriend), and the two of you run into his best friend and his wife. Still frustrated about the

discussion you two had regarding boundaries, your insignificant other decides to discuss your beliefs with the couple. He says, "Nancy has a no-kiss policy! Can you believe that? This is my first time ever hearing anything about that! She literally refuses to kiss me before marriage because she's afraid that we'll end up having sex." With those words, his friend drops his head and giggles, and then, turns and looks at his wife. She says, "Well, Terrance and I kissed before marriage and we didn't have sex. Don't be so uptight. Relax sis! God knows your heart!" It is great that they were able to accomplish this feat, but in all truth, more than 80 percent of Christians (and I'm being nice with this number) wouldn't be able to pull it off! I've advised people and they were able to remain abstinent, which was something they'd never done in their lives, but they went and got advice elsewhere and ended up limping out of some man's bedroom. What works for someone else may not work for you!

8. **Be mindful of your conversations.** In all truth, it's not difficult for a conversation to take a wrong turn, and if you don't recover it within the first few seconds, you can find yourself engaging in phone sex or some other form of soft porn. Some things have to be ignored, for example, your insignificant other may joke and say, "My co-worker said his wife likes to sleep in the nude, even in the winter. I told him, 'Man, I need me a wife like that.'" He follows this up with an uncomfortable chuckle and then a brief moment of

silence. Of course, he's waiting on you to respond, so you laugh and say, "Okay." Not getting the response he wants, he lowers his voice all the more and says, "What about you? What do you sleep in?" Don't answer that question. Guys typically initiate these types of conversations when they're aroused, and if he's aroused, you two probably haven't been saying much on the line for the last few minutes. And this has given him too much time to get lost in his thoughts, especially if it's late at night. Just change the subject. Respond with, "That's not your business yet," and then either get off the phone or start a sobering conversation. Start talking about the presidential election, politics, Harriet Tubman, the war on drugs, the Bubonic plague, COVID-19, Gandhi, the Salem witch trials, world peace—anything anti-sex! If he's playing romantic music in the background, turn on some gospel. That should sober him up!

9. **Be accountable with your boundaries.** This is why it's a good idea to write them down. Share them with your leaders and mentors; this way, they can help you to decide which boundaries are unrealistic and which ones are traps.

10. **Have fun with your boundaries!** In all truth, people nowadays think that boundaries take away all the fun that could be had in a relationship, so when some people read the list above, they'll reason with themselves that if they were to comply with what I've taught, they'd be single for a long time. And guess

what? They may be right! Here's the thing—you have to determine whether you want to be in a relationship or if you are waiting for THE relationship that leads to marriage. Some folks are serial daters; they like the feeling of being pursued so-much-so that they will waste the time of another human being or allow their time to be wasted just so they won't have to be left alone to their own thoughts. In other words, they don't know how to be alone! And I get it! This was a generational curse in my family and I was once a slave to it! But God set me free, and now, I'm content as a single, just as I'll be content whenever I get married. You can have boundaries in relationships and still have a lot of fun! There are tons of couples out there who can attest to this! They remained abstinent and some even waited to share their first kisses at the altar! Thinking that having boundaries is boring is no different than thinking that saved people have no fun. We do. We just do it with our clothes on!

ARRESTING THE SPIRIT OF BONDAGE

Before we go into this lesson, let's get a basic understanding of what a spirit is, after all, some religions and some denominations don't necessarily teach about spirits, spiritual warfare or anything that remotely deals with the spirit realm. The problem with this is—we are all spirits living inside of a body, and if we learn more about the shells (bodies) we're in than we learn about ourselves, we'll spend the rest of our (earthly) lives pacifying our temporal states, rather than catering to our eternal states. So, what is a spirit? Let's look to the scriptures to get an answer. Genesis 2:7 reads, "And the LORD God formed man of the dust of the ground, and breathed into his nostrils the breath of life; and man became a living soul." Let's pull a few keywords out of this scripture.

1. God formed man out of the dust from the ground.
2. God breathed the breath of life into the man's nostrils.
3. Man became a living soul.

These three statements deal with the makeup of humans. Remember, we are tripartite beings, consisting of a body, a soul and a spirit.

- **Body:** The dust of the ground represents the flesh, outer shell or skin of a man.
- **Spirit:** The breath of life is God in the spirit of a man; it is his life force.
- **Soul:** The soul of a man consists of his mind, will and

emotions.

The Greek word for spirit is "pneuma." This is where we get the word "pneumonia," and according to Strong's Concordance, it means: breath, wind, spirit. Therefore, the spirit of a man is his life force; it is the part of him that makes him like God. Remember, we are created in the image and likeness of God. God is Spirit. In other words, He is Life or the Source of life. This is why both angels and humans are eternal creatures. God gave us the breath of life, and because we are eternal creatures, we have to be housed in eternity. This is why He created hell for Satan and his angels; they have to have an eternal abode. Of course, when human beings pass on from this life, we have to spend eternity somewhere, right? There are only two places prepared for eternal creatures; this is why we want to fall on the right side of the spectrum. Howbeit, in short, a spirit is an eternal creature; it is a living, thinking force. So, when we talk about unclean spirits, we are talking about fallen angels; these are the spirits who partnered with Satan and were cast out of Heaven because of their betrayal and their rebellion. They lost their heavenly bodies, so when they were cast out of Heaven (see Revelation 12:9) they became disembodied spirits. A disembodied spirit is a spirit without a body. Please note that these angels were cast into the Earth; this is why they roam about seeking who they may devour. On the other hand, once a human being dies, that person's spirit does not remain on Earth. Ecclesiastes 12:7 confirms this; it reads, "And the dust returns to the earth as it was, and the spirit returns to God who gave it."

When Satan and his angels were cast out of Heaven, they didn't stop operating. Revelation 12:12 reads, "Therefore rejoice, ye heavens, and ye that dwell in them. Woe to the inhabiters of the earth and of the sea! For the devil is come down unto you, having great wrath, because he knoweth that he hath but a short time." Now, Satan and his crew are going about the Earth wreaking havoc everywhere they go. All the same, please don't think they are emotional creatures running rampart and attacking any and everyone that they can. No, the kingdom of darkness is set up like any other kingdom; Satan and his henchmen have an organized and established system, meaning, Satan is very strategic. Every spirit that belongs to that kingdom has a function, an assignment and a rank. This includes the spirit of bondage. How does the spirit of bondage get in? It's simple:

1. God created boundaries. On every side of a boundary, you will find systems. These are the tools and the processes used to carry out specific functions. All of these processes are independent of one another; in other words, they can function alone. All of these processes are interdependent on one another; in other words, they accomplish more whenever they work together. The binding agent for each system is called agreement.

2. On every side of a boundary, you will find legalities and creatures who enforce those legalities. Whenever someone violates a boundary, that person (or spirit)

can and oftentimes will end up bound by those who are assigned to protect the borders of that system. For example, we are citizens of the Kingdom of God, but if we go into sin, Satan and his henchmen will utilize that opportunity to bind us.

3. Once a person is bound, that person will be mentally incarcerated and forced to serve the system that he or she has entered into. For example, a believing woman experiments with drugs. She crosses this boundary a few times before she ends up getting bound or, better yet, addicted to the drugs she's been experimenting with. Now bound, she will find herself constantly thinking about the drugs and how to get more of them. This will eventually lead her to a life of crime and gross sin. In other words, she is now a slave of the system that she kept flirting with.

4. The spirit that binds, monitors and intimidates people is referred to as the spirit of bondage.

The spirit of bondage falls under the fear category, meaning, it works directly with the spirit of fear to carry out its agenda. Healthline reported the following:

"According to a 2009 study published in the European Journal of Social Psychology, it takes 18 to 254 days for a person to form a new habit. The study also concluded that, on average, it takes 66 days for a new behavior to become automatic" (Source: Healthline/How Long Does It Take for a New Behavior to Become Automatic?)

Note: According to Health Line, it takes 18 to 254 days to break a habit as well. Another word for "habit" is "stronghold." What exactly is a stronghold? Lexico gives two definitions for the word "stronghold." They are:

1. A place that has been fortified so as to protect it against attack.
2. A place where a particular cause or belief is strongly defended or upheld.

Remember that the soul has three layers or levels; they are:
- Conscious Mind
- Subconscious Mind
- Unconscious Mind

What is the conscious mind again? It's the waiting room of the soul. The subconscious is, biblically speaking, what we refer to as the heart. This is what God told us to guard. The unconscious mind is the house of our spirit. This is the part that Satan cannot bind, but he can and often does build a siege wall around it if he gets the opportunity. Let's use the woman experimenting with drugs as an example. First and foremost, she's already bound if she's experimenting with drugs. Let's call her Morgan. Morgan is likely bound by the spirit of rejection, which is why she's experimenting with drugs in the first place. She wants to fit in and be accepted by her peers. This means that she's bound in the platonic state, and she is likely bound in the familial state. Chances are, one or both of her parents were physically and/or emotionally absent from her life. She may be bound in the romantic state as well. Her choice of friends may be directly related to her choice in men. She likes tattoo-covered guys who live on the edge, so she surrounds herself with women who she believes are more appealing to these types of guys. It started with one of her roommates in college named Sonya. Sonya had a huge tattoo on her neck, an earlobe gauge in each ear and hair that she'd dyed green and yellow. This particular roommate had a rebellious bad boy of a boyfriend (Richard) who'd gotten to college on a sports scholarship, but he was always living on the edge. He was definitely fun to be around and he was surrounded by the types of guys that Morgan was attracted to, so Morgan went out of her way to impress Sonya. Eventually, this worked and Sonya invited her to a few parties. Everyone at these parties would experiment with drugs and/or alcohol. Not wanting to stand out, Morgan experimented with heroin a few times. It started off with marijuana, but after that, she found herself in a bedroom with a group of ladies about to take heroin for the first time. Before long, she found herself addicted to heroin, and she'd get high just about every day with her new boyfriend, Steve. Steve was exactly the type of man she had been interested in. What happened here? The spirit of rejection invited a few other spirits to the party that it was throwing in her soul; it invited:

1. Fear of rejection
2. Abandonment
3. Fear of abandonment
4. Rebellion
5. Pride

6. Envy

All of these spirits linked together and created the path needed for the spirit of bondage to enter in. This particular spirit is a taskmaster. According to Oxford Languages, a taskmaster is: "a person who imposes a harsh or onerous workload on someone." What workload did she receive? She stole money from her parents, she stole money and property from her roommate, she sold her body and she stole from just about every store she walked into. Eventually, she ended up being arrested and thrown into jail for three months. But this didn't break the spirit of bondage off her life. Instead, when she got out of jail, she reached out to her boyfriend, Steve, who immediately picked her up and took her to a seedy hotel. There, they indulged in heroin and a few other drugs. Please note that once these spirits entered the waiting room of her mind, because she was already bound by rejection, she didn't cast them down or resist them. And once they entered her subconscious, they formed another band around her soul; this hard outer layer is called pride. Pride hardens the heart, making it nearly impenetrable to the truth. This is what it looks like to be bound by the spirit of bondage. She'd crossed a boundary, and consequently, she'd ended up bound in her romantic state. Remember, Satan will advance from one state to the other; that is, until he has his host bound in every area of his or her mind. What does this look like when an empath is bound by a narcissist? The truth of the matter is the empath is not a slave to the narcissistic personality. The empath is a slave to a need he or she has. For one, if you are an empath, you are prophetic; we've already established this. This means that you were specifically created and/or called to serve as a mouthpiece for God. This is why He had to make you super-sensitive; this is why you fall in love easily and this is why you brag about "loving hard." In truth, there's no such thing as "loving hard." What you're saying when you say this is either:

1. You can and often do find yourself in idolatry.
2. You can and often do find yourself bound by what you thought was love. In truth, it's just obsession, co-dependency or lust.
3. You often give people intimate access to your heart, and whenever you do this, you don't know how to let them go whenever they prove to be too broken, too immature or too wicked to have that level of access to you.

There are two ways to love a person; they are:

1. The right way.
2. The wrong way.

When we love people the right way, we don't "possess" them. Instead, we give them the grace, the space, the correction and the information that they'll need to flourish independent of us and interdependently with us. In other words, love is a system. Howbeit, if the person does not love us back, we have to keep loving him or her, but not necessarily with an intimate form of love. For example, love has four levels; they are:

1. Eros (Romantic Love)
2. Philia (Friendly love)
3. Storge (Family love)
4. Agape (God's kind of love/ unconditional love)

Each level of love demands a certain degree of intimacy. It goes without saying that we should love one another with Agape love; we must learn to love one another despite our flaws. You wouldn't give Eros love to a brother in Christ. This is reserved for your husband. If you were dating your brother in Christ, you'd extend Philia and Agape to him, and even then, you would have to guard your heart to ensure that you don't give him a level of access that he has not proven himself to be mature enough to handle. This means that your relationship with him has to remain above the surface; that is, unless the two of you are mature enough and ready to go further into your relationship, meaning, you want to advance towards marriage. This doesn't mean that he would get another level of physical access to you; it simply means that the two of you are forming a tighter bond. This bond consists of agreements that you've made, for example, to court each other exclusively. You'd bring others into this agreement, for example, you'd tell your parents, your children (if they're old enough and mature enough), your pastors and you may even make it public knowledge. In this, you'd be a little more intimate in your discussions, meaning, you'd give him more details about your past and you'd share some of your deepest fears or concerns with him. Howbeit, if the guy has not proven himself to be ready for this level of access and you give it to him already, you've just allowed your belief that he's the one to go from the waiting room to the epicenter of your heart. This is what creates the soul tie. Remember, an ungodly soul tie is a yoke. From this point on, you would work tirelessly to strengthen and maintain the soul tie with this guy. The soul tie will serve as the stronghold; this is the belief or binding agent that holds the two of you together. Remember, a stronghold is "a place where a particular cause or belief is strongly defended or upheld." This would mean that the spirit of bondage has bound you in your romantic state. From there, it will advance towards every other state, oftentimes starting with your financial state, your platonic state and your familial state.

Breaking Out of Financial Bondage

Remember, a demon or an unclean spirit is a disembodied spirit; in short, it is a mind without a body. Its goal is to bind itself to your mind; this way, your thoughts and imaginations would be similar to its thoughts and imaginations. Consequently, you'd do the will of that spirit. But in order to link itself up to your mind, it has to get you to agree with it. How does this happen? It's simple. It attacks you in an area where you lack knowledge, understanding, wisdom and identity. For example, if you lack financial knowledge, the spirit of bondage would overwhelm you with fantasies about material things; these thoughts are designed to get you to spend every dollar that comes into your pocket. We've all seen this, especially those of us who've worked in retail.

Arresting the Spirit of Bondage

When I worked for Walmart, the first of the month was always the busiest day of the month. This is because, at that time, most people on public assistance would get their assistance. Now, before I go any further, let me state the obvious—not everyone who is on public assistance is a slave to the system, but the majority of people who rely on public aid are! All the same, all races benefit from public aid! I was born into that world and I grew up there, surrounded by family members, friends and neighbors who all benefited from getting public assistance. Some people simply fell on hard times, but then there are others who have no plans to come off public aid. This is not because they are physically impaired in any way; the problem is that they have been taught that they are victims. A victim's mentality is a slave mentality. And victims can and will abuse the system. Nevertheless, on the first of the month, every aisle in Walmart would be packed with people grabbing anything from food to television sets, and they would completely wreck the store. It was during the first three days of the month where we'd hear the most profanity, deal with the rudest customers and have to work the longest hours. Below, you'll find a common pattern for people who are in financial bondage.

1. The person would get a direct deposit or some form of currency. Let's pretend that this person is a woman.
2. Regardless of whether she had a need or not, just knowing that she had money at her disposal was enough to make the young lady restless. She would become overwhelmed with thoughts about what she

doesn't have and how it would feel to have it.

3. She would go on a shopping spree, buying the most expensive of foods (steaks, lobsters, shrimp) and frivolously spend money on any and everything that triggers an emotional response in her heart.

4. The individual would go home with bags of food and goodies, and this would create a high of sorts. This is especially true when her children excitedly rush to the car to grab the many bags. This is even heightened if she has a partner at home who excitedly rushes out to help with the bags. This is because days like these are normally stress free and fun! Please note that this feeling is addictive!

5. The woman in question would go into the house and put away everything that she has purchased, but once everyone has settled down and is no longer excited, she would check the balance of her public aid account. If the balance is over a certain amount of money (this differs per person), she would become restless and begin to make more plans for the next day. You see, the way that financial bondage works is, it'll take away your peace whenever there is a surplus in your bank account. And by taking away your peace, I don't mean that it would give you chaotic thoughts. Instead, you'd find yourself constantly thinking about what you don't have. This means the spirit has you on an allowance.

6. The woman would go out the next day and shop some more. This pattern would continue for the next

few days; that is, until the balance on her card is low. This low number would reflect what she is accustomed to having in her account. She would then start talking about being more cautious with spending.

7. She would remember things that she has not gotten, so slowly but surely, she'd spend what's left in her account.

8. Everyone in her household will eat twice the amount of food that they normally eat; this is not because they're hungry. There are two reasons that this happens: For one, it's because they deal with the same pressure that she dealt with when she had a surplus of money in her account. Knowing that there's a lot of food in the kitchen will give them a false sense of hunger. In other words, they'll eat just because the food is there. And secondly, if there are more than two children in the home, most of the children will eat just because they don't want their siblings to eat all the food. In other words, they'll begin to compete. This is especially true if one of the children is constantly in the refrigerator. This causes the other children to think and believe that their brother or sister is going to eat up everything before they have a chance to taste it. Consequently, the children will go and eat food that they're not hungry for. Some will even hide food.

This is what we call a system! It's a pattern and a stronghold, and I can assure you that most of the people who've been a slave to this system can attest to the pointers above. The point is—whenever a person is in financial bondage, the spirit of bondage will attack that person's thoughts and imaginations until he or she has spent up all of his or her money. This also means that this particular spirit is acting as a husband to the bound party. This is why you don't just cast a demon out, you have to divorce it! To divorce it means that you have to confront and dismantle the stronghold that's around your mind. For example, to come out of financial bondage, you should:

1. First and foremost, you have to get past the guards if you want to be set free. These are the guarding spirits that hold you in captivity! Remember, the guarding spirits of a system are fear, false justice, rejection, pride and offense. Let's talk about false justice. Please note that there are people who Heaven labels as defenders; they defend the faith and they defend the poor and the needy. But everything Heaven did, hell mimicked! In other words, there are false defenders out there who will go out of their way to make you feel comfortable in your bondage. These people will shout, for example, "Girl, it's okay! Get your food stamps; you deserve them! Don't listen to all of these folks who have something to say about what you do with your money!" It's not your money. It's money taken from taxpayers, but that's another story. The point is—don't listen to people who stir you up emotionally, but can't give you any real solutions other than to encourage you to remain emotional and rebellious. These people are cheerleaders for the

spirit of pride, which is another guarding spirit. Get past them so that you can embrace the truth that's sitting in the waiting room of your soul!

2. Give yourself an expiration date to be on public aid; that is, if you're on it. You can say, "I'll give myself three months to stop relying on the system. No excuses!"

3. Get a full-time job, but also be sure to build your career. Never settle for minimum wage! Never settle for earning just enough money to make ends meet. Let God introduce you to your potential. Please note that if you settle for little money, chances are, you'll return to being a slave of the system. This is because the common mode of reasoning for people who have not furthered their education is—"Why would I get a job and work for the same amount that I could be getting just sitting at home?!" This is especially true when that person comes across a problematic co-worker.

4. Commit to not quitting that job, no matter how hard it gets! Many people who are slaves to the system are genuinely strong people, but the problem is, they don't know their strength. They've watched their parents quit everything that triggered them negatively. Consequently, they themselves don't know how to deal with their rawest emotions. For example, people who are slaves to the system are often said to be loud, regardless of what race and nationality they are! This is because the system muzzles them; it makes

their voices irrelevant, and in an attempt to be heard, many people bound by poverty can be both loud and emotional.

5. Go to college or do something to build/further your career.
6. Resist the overwhelming temptation to spend every dollar that touches your hand. Create a savings account and put some money away.
7. Get financial literacy. A great ministry to follow for this is Dave Ramsey's ministry.
8. Go to some of the most expensive neighborhoods in your town and look at some of the empty houses. If you can tour them, do so! This opens your mind to another world!
9. Surround yourself with people who are financially sound, and whatever you do, do NOT borrow money from them! It can and does take time to build relationships with people who are financially mature when you are financially immature. The reason for this is—financially immature people are always asking to borrow money and expecting their more stable friends to pick up the tab. This sends the message to their friends that they are paying for the friendship. Don't do this! Pick up the tab sometimes. Make sure that the friendship is balanced; this way, you can learn from the people in your circle.
10. Ask the Lord for help. If you truly want to be free, He will help you to push past everything that would hold you in bondage; this way, you can manifest the

potential He's placed in you.

Breaking Out of Romantic Bondage

Remember, we can be free in some states, but bound in others. Every state of a man borders another state. Satan knows this; this is what has helped him to be effective in many of his attacks. For example, let's create a character who we'll call Leroy. Ever since Leroy was in his mother's womb, he has been under a spiritual attack. His mother took pills on three separate occasions when she was pregnant with him in her attempt to abort him. This was because Leroy's father had rejected her and refused to acknowledge himself as the father of the child she was carrying at that time. Broken, alone and broke, she'd decided that she did not want to be a mother, so she'd taken a lot of painkillers, hoping they'd kill her unborn child. This hadn't worked, so whenever she gave birth to Leroy, she simply could not bond with him. She neglected him, abused him and put all of her boyfriends before him. When Leroy turned 14-years old, he committed his first crime. He'd shot his mother's live-in boyfriend in the arm. Because of this, Leroy was sent to juvenile detention until he was 16-years old. After that, he was released into the custody of his grandmother. His grandmother wasn't much of an upgrade from his mother. She didn't have a boyfriend because of her hatred towards men, but what she did have was a foul mouth and a pretty impressive gun collection. And within a few months of living there, Leroy would find himself homeless again after he'd gotten in trouble at school for fighting. His grandmother then surrendered him to the state where he remained until his 18th birthday. All the same, every attempt of Leroy to reach his father had been futile. So, it goes without saying that Leroy is both under-developed and damaged in the parental state. But he's a good-looking and pretty intelligent kid.

Leroy finally graduates from high school and goes on to become a mechanic. Nevertheless, his striking good looks, his boldness and his charismatic personality makes him the center of attention just about everywhere that he goes. And it goes without saying that by the time Leroy turned 22-years old, he'd already had three children with three women. And just like his father, he isn't that present of a force in two of his children's lives; this is because they are girls and he has a major problem with women. He sees them as manipulative and wicked. But his third child is a boy. Because he has a son, Leroy goes and reconciles with the mother of his son so that he can be present and active in his son's life. Nevertheless, three years into their relationship, the couple break up after Leroy's girlfriend gives birth to a little girl. Again, Leroy does not bond with his daughter. Instead, he begs his ex-girlfriend to let him come and pick up his son from time-to-time, but she refuses. She's angry with him because he ended the relationship with her, plus, he hasn't been active in their daughter's life.

Five years later, Leroy meets a woman named Michelle. Michelle is a Christian woman who loves the Lord and is in the process of getting her ministerial license. Nevertheless, Michelle is immature. The evidence of this is the fact that she exchanged numbers with Leroy and she'd agreed to start a relationship with him. This is because, like many believing women, she thinks that she can "help" Leroy to become the man that God designed him to be, after all, Leroy opened up to her and told her about his childhood. This led her to believe that she could "fix" and save Leroy. All the same, Michelle had a history of her own. While her father had been present in her life and he'd acknowledged her as his daughter, he had also been unpredictable and distant. His wife hadn't liked Michelle, so Michelle's father would be in and out of her life. Her mother had done the best that she could with what she knew, but she'd worked two jobs, meaning, she was rarely home. Because of this, Michelle had to raise herself and her younger siblings. So, it goes without saying that Michelle experienced rejection as well, but not as deeply as Leroy had. Plus, Leroy has never had a relationship that didn't involve sex. The concept of sex before marriage was not only foreign to him, but it was offensive. So, after three months of dating, the couple engaged in a sexual relationship. This was because Michelle could sense that Leroy was starting to pull away from her. Fearful of losing him, she'd invited him over to her place where the couple ended up having their first sexual encounter. Michelle justified this with the fact that not only had her and Leroy talked about marriage, they'd pretty much set a date. The couple continued in their relationship, and eleven months later, they exchanged vows at the local

12

courthouse. Eight months later, Michelle gave birth to—you guessed it—a baby girl! In truth, the couple had known they were having a girl six months before the child was born. They'd even had a gender reveal, and whenever they'd seen pink confetti coming out of their gender reveal cannons, Leroy could barely hide his disappointment. He'd thrown his cannon to the ground and proceeded to walk away; that is, until one of his uncles was able to calm him down. And now, they were the parents of a seven-pound baby girl who looked just like Leroy's mother. She was the spitting image of her grandmother! Not long after this, Michelle discovered that Leroy was still sleeping with his ex-girlfriend and had gotten her pregnant. If this wasn't bad enough, another girl was now claiming to be pregnant by Leroy as well, but this particular girl was no stranger to Michelle. She was Michelle's 18-year old niece, Lydia. She'd met Leroy at the gender reveal party and the two of them had immediately started an affair. It goes without saying that Michelle and Leroy ended up divorcing, and Leroy went on to have eight more children with eight additional women.

Every state borders another one. Leroy was wounded in his parental state. Again, this state borders our romantic states. He was also wounded and bound financially and platonically. He did not know how to have friendships with people of the opposite sex! To him, a woman was nothing more than an opportunity for him to momentarily escape his rejection. But let's get back to Michelle. She's hurting, she's angry and she's now a divorced mother of one who has been romantically humiliated by her ex-husband. If that's not bad enough, Leroy is perpetuating the same cycle of abandonment that he'd endured as a child. He wants absolutely nothing to do with his daughter. He even had his attorney to ask Michelle's attorney if he could sign away his parental rights. In truth, Leroy is a narcissistic and broken soul, and everyone who tries to love him pays for this dearly. This includes Michelle's niece, Lydia, who also goes on to give birth to a baby girl, only to discover that Leroy wants nothing to do with her or her daughter. Thankfully for her, DNA would eventually prove that Leroy was not the father of her daughter; instead, the father turned out to be her obsessed ex's child. With this, we find several people in romantic bondage. Again, Satan advanced on them romantically by first entering their parental states. What they'd endured with their parents deformed their thinking about the opposite sex. It also deformed how they saw God. Whenever we have father issues, those wounds often distort our perception of God, thus, causing us to humanize Him. And while Michelle may stand in front of her church family praying for God to make her whole, what she has to understand is wholeness is the direct result of us personally doing the work needed to fix ourselves, otherwise, we'll use people as human bandages. Remember, she thought that she could fix Leroy when she was the one who needed restoration. Consequently, a broken woman attracted an even more broken man, and that man damaged her all the more. Now, Leroy has left a trail of babies who will grow up without a father, having to wrestle with the spirit of rejection.

And if these children are not healed and restored, they will go on to perpetuate the same cycles. They will find themselves damaged in their parental states as well as their romantic states. This will impact them financially as well. Can you imagine the amount of child support that Leroy has to pay each month? All the same, if Michelle doesn't do the work needed and do something with her life other than being a cashier, taxpayers will continue to pay for her poor choices. This can and will impact her ministry, after all, how can we teach against a system that we are dependent on?

It goes without saying that the million dollar question is—how do we break out of romantic bondage? I remember being 17-years old and suffering through my very first case of heartbreak. All the way up until that point, I'd managed to not give my heart away to a boy. Instead, I had boyfriends, but I wasn't silly enough to believe that they'd be life partners. I just took it one day at a time with them, but when I'd turned 17, I'd met a guy who was nothing like any boy I'd ever dated. As a matter of fact, my mother adored him. And because she accepted him, I stopped guarding my heart. I believed that he would be my husband and I believed that he would never hurt me. Oh how young and naive I was! When we broke up, he managed to make me feel like I was the one breaking up with him when, in truth, I had simply confronted him about his indiscretions. I wasn't saved back then and I didn't know what to do with all of my teenage emotions, after all, I had never experienced the effects of a broken heart. So, about two months after our breakup, I actually called a psychic hotline to ask a medium whether or not me and my ex would get back together. I was a complete mess! The witch on the other end was nothing more than a normal woman working a job. She told me that my ex and I would get back together, marry and have children. She said what I wanted to hear at that time! I hung up the line, and another lie advanced from the waiting room of my heart and entered into my subconscious. From there, I found myself bound to the belief that he was the proverbial "one" for another two years. But what helped me to get free from the belief that I could rely on a witch for a word was the day when my mother couldn't find her car keys. She was frantically looking for them and she believed that me or my siblings had something to do with their disappearance, so she was screaming at the top of her lungs. To make matters worse, she was running late for work, so she was in a hurry to find her keys. I don't remember what threat she gave us, but what I do remember was being terrified. So, in a complete frantic, I picked up the phone and called that same psychic hot-line that I'd called a few months prior. I lowered my voice so my mother wouldn't hear me on the phone because if she knew that I had called another 900 number, she would have beat me within an inch of my life. I said to the woman on the other end, "My mother's keys are missing. Can you tell me where they are?" I could tell that this was one of those calls that she dreaded. She didn't know what to say, so she said something that completely delivered me from relying on psychics. She said, "Trace your footsteps and you will find the keys." What?! I was extremely upset. I immediately disconnected the phone. Why was I risking my life to call a line that charged $3.99 a minute just to hear someone tell me what I could have told myself? Almost immediately after I hung up, my brother announced that he'd found my mother's keys. Trace your footsteps—26 years later, I still remember those words as if I'd just heard them yesterday. But while she didn't give me any divine advice, she had echoed the words of every person who'd ever stood near me when I'd lost something. What does this mean? It simply means to come out of romantic bondage, you must look at where you've been to understand just where you are. Why did Michelle think that she could fix Leroy? To answer this question, Michelle would have to look at her past, and in doing so, she would soon discover that:

1. She's a woman (obviously). A woman is a man with a womb. In other words, women take potential and try to incubate it, hoping that they could give birth to something great. Leroy, like every man on the face of this planet, had potential. Michelle saw his potential and thought that she had what it took to take in a wounded boy and give birth to a whole man. This is called deception. She was in the wilderness of her potential, meaning, she was immature. Consequently, she attracted a wild animal.

2. She didn't have the tools to fix a broken soul. Leroy would have to want Jesus and he would have to personally pursue Him in order to get healed, delivered and restored. Michelle did not possess the ability to drag that man to the cross!

3. She was using Leroy as a void-filler. This means that she's not the victim in this equation. Despite how narcissistic and broken Leroy was, Michelle served as a predator in his life. She didn't honor God's Word, so she didn't bring any sanctity to the name of Jesus. Instead, she took in a man who needed Jesus and tried to evangelize him in the bedroom. She made herself and other believers common to Leroy. Wildlife experts often tell us not to feed the animals. The reason for this is because it causes them to lose their fear of humans, but it does not and cannot rid the animal of its instincts. So, if I'm feeding an alligator, that same gator can walk up to another woman looking to be fed. If she does not feed it or if she gets too close, that animal would turn her into its meal. Now, I'm not speaking of Leroy in a condescending way, after all, he is a broken soul who needs Jesus just like I do. I'm dealing more with his thinking patterns. He is animalistic in his ways and in this thinking. And because Michelle went after him, it would be harder for another evangelist to win his soul for the Lord because Michelle served as a spiritual pedophile in his life. All the same, she left a bad taste in Leroy's mouth regarding Christians, since she was always berating him about his worldly ways.

4. Leroy could not and would never fix her father wounds. She first needed to truly reconcile her relationship with Father God before she even looked at the idea of a relationship. Now, you may say that

she is in a good space with God because she's pursuing a ministerial license, but titles don't equate to good fruit! God said that you will know them by their fruits; this is what a man or woman produces. Michelle produced a toxic relationship because she wasn't mature enough for marriage, which meant that she wasn't mature enough for certain levels of ministry or platforms in ministry. She also needed to get counseling regarding her relationship with her natural father.

5. She could not hijack her next season! A season represents a space in time when our minds have been renewed. It is a mindset, and not an event! Her mind clearly hadn't been renewed yet, so she could not morally or legally enter her next season without destroying it. Remember what a loan is—it is borrowing from your future. It means to place the future you in bondage just to receive some relief today. This is what it looks like when we attempt to hijack our next seasons; when we attempt to be wives when we haven't yet mastered being daughters. We essentially rob the future versions of ourselves of peace and much of what we could have potentially had if we had made better choices today. In essence, we place our future selves in bondage to unforgiveness, hurt, rejection, being a single parent and all that comes with a toxic relationship in exchange for pleasure and a sense of acceptance today.

But how do we come out of romantic bondage? It's simple. Trace your footsteps. Look at the history of every one of your states and undo the damage that has been done to them. You do this through:

1. **Deliverance:** this casts the devils out of those states.
2. **Therapy:** this deals with the damage done to those states. Therapists sweep away the dirt and debris of yesterday.
3. **Accountability:** share your thoughts, fears and dreams with someone who (1) loves the Lord and (2) is in the place that you're trying to arrive at. Ask the Lord to send you a mentor who you can be accountable with, but please note that mentors are designed to circumcise you. This means that your mentor will occasionally correct you. Note: there's a difference between circumcision and castration. The difference is—circumcision prepares you for your assignment, but castration makes it impossible for you to reproduce. Someone who is castrating you will be surrounded by unproductive people; someone who is circumcising you will be surrounded by emotionally healthy and productive people. All the same, the Word tells us that we will know them by their fruits.
4. **Fasting and prayer:** Believe it or not, you need God in every state of your being. This is why you have to spend time in prayer, confessing your sins, fears, insecurities and desires to God; this is so that He can deliver you. Fasting brings the flesh under subjection; this allows you to be led by God's Spirit more

255

effectively.

5. **Study:** You need information! You were formed, but in order for you to be transformed, you need to be informed! Knowledge is the key to your deliverance, and remember, in all your getting, get understanding. This means don't just seek to know what the Bible says, ask God to give you understanding! And lastly, wisdom is the principle thing. In other words, you have to apply what you've learned. Wisdom is a manifestation of what you've learned through your choices and conversations; this allows God to give you revelation. Study to show yourself approved for whatever it is that you've been praying for.

Additionally, please note the following:

1. Don't date or court until you're mature enough to date or court.
2. Be accountable with your relationships.
3. Change your phone number! Your exes should not have access to you.
4. Stop visiting your exes' profiles on social media. Stop visiting your exes' significant or insignificant others and their exes on social media. Move on!
5. Respect every boundary that God has put in place for you. This is what keeps you safe. Remember, if you step outside of a boundary, it's only a matter of time before you get bound.

Bound No More

I'm sure by now that you know what the term "arrested development" means. If not, the Collins Dictionary defines it as "Psychological development that is not complete." It simply means that a human being plateaued too early in life, oftentimes because of trauma or parental neglect. Scientists even believe that most people with narcissistic personality disorder were broken or made to be narcissistic by the time they were three-years old. Consequently, most narcissists are emotionally and mentally immature, which is why they display childlike behaviors whenever they are confronted. Nevertheless, Satan wants to impact us at some age or stage in our development; this way, we can become stuck. All the same, he can normalize dysfunction and toxicity to us. Why do you think it was (or is) so hard to minister to and/or help a man or a woman who is over sixty years old and, as the older people used to say, "stuck in their ways?" You're expecting a light to come on and for your elderly aunt or uncle to understand what you're saying. You lay the evidence in front of them, play the YouTube videos and break down the information in the most simplistic terms, and after you think you've made your point, your relative will blankly and coldly look you in the face and proudly stand by his or her beliefs. But what you may be dealing with is a relative who is stuck; you may be trying to give meat to someone who can barely drink milk. It's too much for the person! Yes, this includes your narcissistic lovers, parents and siblings. In order for them to get free, they need more than a traditional deliverance session; they need years of information! They need to taste and see that the Lord is good. In other words, they have to experience His goodness for themselves! And get this—the same is true for you!

In your parental state, you may be 55-years old; in other words, you may be mature, sound and well put together. On the other hand, financially speaking, you may be an infant who has to be carried by taxpayers and anyone who is willing to help you out. You don't overcome poverty by getting a better job, you overcome poverty by getting a financial education and then applying what you've learned—consistently! Think of our school system. Education comes in layers. You won't listen to a single Dave Ramsey podcast and get instant deliverance! No, you need to flood, overwhelm and immerse your mind in information. This means that you have to study, study and study some more! And not just study, you have to research what you study to get a deeper understanding of it. Once you have addressed every state of yourself, the enemy will find no place (opportunity) in you. All the same, you have to absolutely respect the boundaries put in place by God and by man. Some of man's boundaries are solid, but some will also be unreasonable and unrealistic. Nevertheless, you still have to honor them as long as they don't intrude upon your own boundaries. And when you do this, you'll have peace on every side. This is especially true if you study and honor the Word of God. He told us to not be unequally yoked with unbelievers, to deliver ourselves from the hands of the fowler (debtors), to seek the Kingdom of Heaven and all His righteousness first, to present our bodies as living sacrifices holy and acceptable to Him, to love Him with all of our hearts, souls and minds, to love our neighbors (not neighborhoods) as we love ourselves, to pray without ceasing, to be angry but sin not, to forgive our enemies, and the list goes on. If we study, honor and apply His Word in our lives, Satan will be rendered powerless against us. Nevertheless, you may already be in the depths of a ditch that you dug for yourself or one that you were born in. The million dollar question then becomes—how do I get out of this mess? Before I list the pointers, let me give you this disclaimer. What I share with you may not necessarily be what you want to hear. As a leader, a teacher, a coach and a mentor, I've come to understand that many people seek confirmation, not information. For example, a woman tolerating an abusive, promiscuous and narcissistic boyfriend oftentimes doesn't want to hear that she needs to love herself enough to walk away from the relationship she's in. Instead, she is on the prowl, looking for counselors and teachers who will teach her a few tricks and trades that she can use to coerce, provoke or even force her boyfriend to honor his relationship with her. In other words, what she wants to hear and what she needs to hear are not one and the same. Below, you'll find how to deliver yourself from the narcissist, the toxic individual and how to deliver you from yourself!

1. **Heal.** Every wound in your life will serve as a void, and remember, voids have what can best be described as a gravitational pull. In other words, hurt

people tend to attract hurt people, and these people aren't coming to restore, they are coming to relate. Get as much therapy as you'll need to become the best version of yourself possible.

2. **Forgive.** This includes you forgiving yourself! All too often, our anger towards people is rooted in the fact that they made us angry with ourselves. They explored and exploited one of our weaknesses, thus, making us self-conscious and insecure. Remember, every person you come in contact with has a certain level of information, a certain degree of understanding and a certain measure of maturity. God didn't say you will know them by their titles, He said that you would know them by their fruits! Looking at the fruits of a person will tell you everything you need to know about that person, and of course, the fruits He's mentioning are the fruits of the Holy Spirit or the fruits (works) of the flesh—whichever ones are present and reproducing themselves in that person's life. If you allowed someone to get too close without you observing that person's fruits, take accountability for your wrong, forgive the person, forgive yourself and draft up a blueprint of how you plan to manage yourself in the future.

3. **Set boundaries and enforce them**—consistently and without apology! Narcissists hate boundaries because Satan hates boundaries. Find a writing apparatus and write down some of the violations and offenses people tend to make towards you. List those

people's names and the tactics that they use to get what they want from you. After this, list ways that you plan to combat this in the future. Communicate your boundaries to these people and then give yourself a hefty penalty for every time you allow that person to cross that boundary. For example, if I had a friend who only called me when she wanted to talk, and she'd take over the conversation, only stopping to acknowledge something I said every few minutes, I would make it a point to (1) not answer all of her calls (2) communicate with her about her ways (3) interrupt the conversation so that I can speak as well, stopping her from time-to-time to say, "You're doing it again; you're dominating the conversation" and (4) give $100 to my charity of choice anytime I allowed her to dominate a conversation and then rush off the phone.

4. **Honor God's Word.** This is your shield; this is your hiding place! Don't let Satan tempt you outside the will of God with empty promises of giving you every one of your heart's desires. Remember this—Satan isn't just a liar, but he's the father of all lies. Don't trust a serpent with your future! All the same, God said that when He blesses us, He will add no sorrow to it (see Proverbs 10:22). I'd rather be blessed with a 2500 square foot home in a middle-class section that was gifted to me by God than to live in a mansion that is pretty much being leased to me by the devil. Satan doesn't give you anything freely. Nothing! Everything he does, both minor and major, comes with a hefty

price tag. And remember, one of his favorite devices is to give you what you desire today in exchange for your future.

5. **Let people walk away!** I can't emphasize this enough! When you start setting and enforcing boundaries, you will see a shift in your relationships. The wrong people will put you on punishment, and if this punishment doesn't teach you a lesson, they'll begin a mass exodus right out of your life. What's crazy about narcissistic and toxic people is they'll convince themselves and others that they are the victims when this is not true. They'll even convince you that they are the victims. Let them walk away, don't chase them, and make it a point to heal. Also understand when many narcissistic people walk out of your life, they won't close the door between themselves and you entirely. They will often keep you on their social media pages; that is, if you don't delete them, and they may even send you a text message every now and then. The reason for this is (1) they are not trying to leave you, most of the time, they are trying to put you on punishment. This punishment can last for weeks and years on end; that is, until you finally become so lonely and desperate that you apologize to them for not allowing them to be as toxic as they are. This would allow them to resume their narcissistic ways in your life without interruption. (2) They want to monitor your life; this allows them to suddenly reappear whenever they see something

great on the horizon for you or laugh whenever and if ever they see calamity making its rounds in your life. (3) Just in case they ever need you for something, and lastly, (4) so they can sabotage your blessings. Understand this—as nice as they can be, as helpful as they can be and as effective as they can be, some people are simply not called to you! What's worse is, many of them are the weapons that were formed against you. But God sees what you don't see and He knows what you refuse to embrace; this is why He will oftentimes perform an enema on your life, driving out every enemy who dares to call himself or herself a friend. This deliverance is oftentimes painful and taxing, but it is necessary!

6. **Walk away!** If the toxic people in your life refuse to walk away, you need to take the initiative to rid yourself of them. Have some hard conversations with people, change your phone number and remove them from your social media pages. But don't put them on punishment or attempt to change them by walking out of their lives. This is psychological witchcraft! When and if you walk away, do so because it's necessary! Never treat the hearts of people like revolving doors, even if those people are broken. As a matter of fact, the most dangerous man or woman is a broken one who has somebody playing with his or her mind. Walk away and heal!

7. **Change!** You must become both what you want and need in a person. One thing you'll soon discover is

that many of the people you've tolerated in your life were there because you had a need that you were too afraid, too content or too lazy to address. Confront and overcome your fears and let God fill your voids. Voids are black holes in the soul that have a huge gravitational pull, meaning, they pull in hardhearted people who also have voids. Imagine this—the man or woman that you've chosen for yourself may simply be there because you are serving as a bandage and a void-filler in that person's life. If that individual were to get healed, delivered and made whole, you would no longer have a place in his or her heart because the void that you once served in has been filled. Consequently, the man or woman that you're with would have to find another place for you in his or her life. If you haven't been made whole, you would then serve as a deficit to that person's life.

8. **Grow up!** Galatians 4:1-3 reads, "Now I say, That the heir, as long as he is a child, differeth nothing from a servant, though he be lord of all; but is under tutors and governors until the time appointed of the father. Even so we, when we were children, were in bondage under the elements of the world." Who is the heir? He (or she) is the child of a dignitary, which means that the person has an inheritance. Nevertheless, as long as the heir is a child, meaning, as long as the individual is immature, that person is no different than a slave. Instead, the scripture tells us that the individual will be under tutors and governors; these

are pastors, leaders, mentors and elders—these are people who help to grow the individual until he or she reaches maturity. The time appointed by the father is not a chronos event; instead, when our Father God sees that we are ready for what we've been praying for, He then opens the windows of Heaven so that we can receive it. In this, you need mentors and/or leaders who can intentionally and consistently inspect, prune and grow you. Please note that the pruning process can be frustrating, offensive at times and scary. Nevertheless, it separates the hungry from the entitled.

9. **No more arrested development.** Get healed and fulfilled in those areas that have been stunted in growth because of trauma, rejection or abandonment. Of course, you do this through counseling and education.

10. **Accept your assignment in Christ.** Please note that being in ministry doesn't mean that you've surrendered to the will of God for your life. It is possible to be in ministry and be outside the will of God. How so? If you're ministering while wearing a muzzle, meaning, you are too afraid to preach the uncompromising truth out of fear that your peers won't accept you, you have not accepted your assignment. You've accepted the title, but not the mantle. Take the muzzle off and be led by the Holy Spirit. Now, this does not mean that you can rebel against your pastor's instructions, after all, God will give you

pastors after His own heart. However, you have to allow Him to lead you through them. This means that sometimes they may tell you to sit down when you feel like you have a lot to say; they may tell you to speak when you feel like you don't have anything to say. This is discipleship. In order for you to become a true disciple of Christ, you need to be disciplined.

Breaking the cords of bondage means breaking the ungodly soul ties, forgiving everyone who's hurt or disappointed you and releasing any and everyone who you've been using to fill your voids. Broken people often use other people to make them feel better about themselves! Make sure that you are a blessing to everyone who is in your life. Remember, you will reap whatever it is that you sow. Breaking the cords of bondage also means you finally coming to terms with who you are in Christ Jesus. If you identify yourself as an empath, chances are, you are wired to be prophetic. Prophetic people are spiritually sensitive because God created them that way; this is so that they could sense and respond to His presence. But again, Satan loves to hijack people that don't know who they are. In other words, your greatest enemy isn't Satan, it's a lack of identity. Satan comes to tell you who he wants you to be, not who you really are. Most empaths truly don't know who they are. The secular world can tell them about their psychology, but cannot help them to understand the spiritual implications behind their identities. Consequently, most of them never come to know why they keep attracting the Jezebel spirit in their lives. You see, having this knowledge would help the empath to break free of the narcissist because it will provoke the individual to search the heart of God all the more. In this, he or she will find more about God and simultaneously discover themselves in the process. In doing so, the empath would look at all of the sentences that he or she has served and strategically end the conversation between themselves and hell by putting a period at the ends of those sentences. This moment of discovery will always mark a major shift in the prophetic individual's life, thus allowing him or her to repent (turn around) and chase the One who can not only fill his or her voids, but can heal it. For example, in 2014, when I started having a series of dreams, God showed me two things:

1. He had delivered me from the life I'd chosen for myself and the demons that came with it.
2. He was preparing me for my assignment in Him. My desire to be the bride of a man would be healed as I married my assignment. This did not mean that I would never marry; it simply meant that the generational curse of not knowing how to be alone was broken.

I was already aware of and serving in my assignment by then, but there was still so much more to God that I did not know, which meant that there was so much more about me that I did not know. There is something incredibly satisfying about God-discovery and self-discovery. It's an exciting, exhilarating and sometimes overwhelming process. Howbeit, it returns to you something that Satan may have stolen from you while you were yet in your mother's womb; that is your voice. Your voice is connected to your identity. It is your voice that allows you to speak to every void in your life, and say what God said after He'd created the Earth—"Let there be light!" In other words, let there be revelation, let there be understanding and let there be systems that reproduce Heaven on Earth. You got this because God's got you! Be free, break free and then whenever you're ready, go and set someone else free!

Prayer to Break the Spirit of Bondage

Father God,

I acknowledge Your presence today. You said in James 1:5, "If any of you lacks wisdom, let him ask God, who gives generously to all without reproach, and it will be given him." Lord, I ask that You give me wisdom. Teach me more about You and teach me more about my assignment in You. I repent for my sins, both known and unknown, and I ask for Your forgiveness. I repent for the sins of my parents, grandparents and ancestors, and I ask that You forgive them. Please set me free from every ungodly soul tie and yoke that has ensnared me. I surrender to Your will for my life. Help me to embrace my assignment in You. Surround me with the right people, send me to the right church, and speedily deliver me from any person, group or organization who is antithetical to my assignment. I ask that you heal my heart, fill my voids and open my ears to hear from You.

I renounce the spirit of bondage and every unclean spirit that is operating in my life, and I command those spirits to leave me now in the name of Jesus Christ! Satan, I renounce you and your assignment for me. I divorce every unclean spirit that you have assigned to my life, and I command those spirits to go to the feet of Christ Jesus and never return to me! You have no place in my life, so leave me now, in Jesus name!

YAHWEH, I ask that you set me free and station your warring and ministering angels around me to aid in this deliverance. Don't allow the enemy to resist my command. And Lord, I ask that You give me a fresh infilling of Your Holy Spirit. I ask these things in the name of Jesus Christ. Amen and Amen.

A Note to the Empath and the Prophetic Individual

Hollywood has not only normalized witchcraft, it has even popularized it. Howbeit, God is passionately against this dark art because it promotes humans to play around in the spirit realm without the clearance and the guidance of the Holy Spirit. Consequently, these people begin to knowingly and unknowingly communicate with fallen angels. These were the angels that were cast out of Heaven along with Satan. Let's look at a few scriptures.

Leviticus 19:31: Regard not them that have familiar spirits, neither seek after wizards, to be defiled by them: I am the LORD your God.

Leviticus 20:6: And the soul that turneth after such as have familiar spirits, and after wizards, to go a whoring after them, I will even set my face against that soul, and will cut him off from among his people.

Leviticus 20:27: A man also or woman that hath a familiar spirit, or that is a wizard, shall surely be put to death: they shall stone them with stones: their blood shall be upon them.

1 Samuel 15:23: For rebellion is as the sin of witchcraft, and stubbornness is as iniquity and idolatry. Because thou hast rejected the word of the LORD, he hath also rejected thee from being king.

Isaiah 8:19-20: And when they shall say unto you, Seek unto them that have familiar spirits, and unto wizards that peep, and that mutter: should not a people seek unto their God? for the living to the dead? To the law and to the testimony: if they speak not according to this word, it is because there is no light in them.

Galatians 5:19-21: Now the works of the flesh are manifest, which are these; Adultery, fornication, uncleanness, lasciviousness, idolatry, witchcraft, hatred, variance, emulations, wrath, strife, seditions, heresies, envyings, murders, drunkenness, revellings, and such like: of the which I tell you before, as I have also told you in time past, that they which do such things shall not inherit the kingdom of God.

1 Chronicles 10:13: So Saul died for his transgression which he committed against the LORD, even against the word of the LORD, which he kept not, and also for asking counsel of one that had a familiar spirit, to inquire of it; and inquired not of the LORD: therefore he slew him, and turned the kingdom unto David the son of Jesse.

Revelation 21:8: But the fearful, and unbelieving, and the abominable, and murderers, and whoremongers, and sorcerers, and idolaters, and all liars, shall have their part in the lake which burneth with fire and brimstone: which is the second death.

Again, turning to sorcery is turning to unclean spirits; these spirits are the enemies of God, and not only this, they want God's people to rely on them and to worship them. The ultimate goal is to turn our hearts away from God. This is why you cannot be a Christian witch; it's an oxymoron. God will not partner with demons, and He has not changed His mind about this. Remember, these are the spirits that were cast out of Heaven along with Satan. Revelation 12:7-9 tells the story; it reads, "And there was war in heaven: Michael and his angels fought against the dragon; and the dragon fought and his angels, and prevailed not; neither was their place found any more in heaven. And the great dragon was cast out, that old serpent, called the Devil, and Satan, which deceiveth the whole world: he was cast out into the earth, and his angels were cast out with him." So, regardless of what Hollywood promotes, when a person consults with a spirit, that person is not in communication with a deceased person. This includes mediums and sorcerers. Now, I didn't say that these people know that they are not in communion with the dead because many of them genuinely believe that they are. One of the reasons for this is because the spirits they are communicating with claim the identities of people who have passed on, and these spirits oftentimes know things that only the deceased parties knew. This is why God said that Satan deceived the whole world. But how do these spirits know things that only a deceased person knew? It's simple. Spirits are timeless; in other words, they are eternal. And just like God assigns angels to watch over us (see Psalms 91:11), Satan assigns demons to monitor our movements. The goal is for those demons to not only monitor our movements, but look for entry points and opportunities to enter our lives. This is why the Bible tells us to give no place to the devil. The word "place" in this context means "opportunity." For example, if you are single and you plan to wait until marriage to have sex, that's wonderful, but those plans can be interrupted if you don't use wisdom. If you allow the man or the woman who you are dating to come into your house, you are playing Russian Roulette with your abstinence. Most people who do this fall into sexual sin. This is because they underestimated the power of a moment. And when Satan sees a believing woman entertaining a believing man in private, he seizes the opportunity to tempt them.

But let's get back to the question. How is it that a medium can accurately tell a person something that only that person's deceased loved one knew? Again, Satan assigns his angels to us, just like he did with our parents, great-grandparents and ancestors. Familiar spirits are called familiar for a reason. They have been in a bloodline for several generations, and they have tempted and overcome many of our predecessors. So, in short, those demons were there the day that great-grandmother buried her wedding ring next to a tree on an abandoned lot. They were there when our great-grandfathers had affairs and produced children in those relationships. They were there when a killer took the life of someone in your ancestral pool and buried that person's body; this is why they can accurately tell you the location of a body. They were there when your great-great aunt had an affair that produced a child with someone other than her husband. They were in the truck with many of us when our parents had heart-to-heart conversations with us. To be absent from the body is to be present with the Lord, meaning, the dead are not walking around this Earth. If an entity manifests itself in your home or wherever you may be, and it disguises itself as one of your deceased loved ones, it is a familiar spirit! It has nothing but evil intentions. This is why you have to bind it and cast it into the abyss. And if you are not convinced that this is an evil spirit, simply say, "I plead the blood of Jesus" and watch what it does. It will disappear!

Why am I discussing this with you? It's simple. Because empaths are spiritually sensitive and oftentimes fall into the traps of idolatry and witchcraft. This is because most empaths don't know who they are! Like our predecessors, we often accept whatever information has been popularized in our eras. Consequently, we end up attracting people who are demonized. And when a person is spiritually sensitive, but has little to no knowledge of God, that person will start looking for answers to questions like:

1. Why do I have vivid dreams that oftentimes come true?
2. Why is it that I can accurately discern the character, motives and intentions of a person when everyone

else seems to be accepting of that person?

3. Why is it that I've experienced moments where I felt a strong urge, for example, to go in a direction other than the direction I normally go in, only to later discover that there was a massive accident in that area around the time when I would have been over that way?

4. How is it that I got a bad feeling in my gut about a guy, so I broke up with him or avoided him, only to later find out that he raped or killed someone?

5. Why do I sometimes know things that others don't know?

Again, a lot of this information may be being filtered to you by a familiar spirit, and get this, it's not trying to protect you, it's trying to earn your trust. Then again, you're likely prophetic; you are sensitive to the voice of God and the presence of His angels. Maybe it was one of His angels who warned and protected you, after all, this is literally what many of them have been assigned to do. But if you don't know the Bible and you don't have an intimate relationship with the Lord, you won't know this. Instead, it would be easy for you to look for answers online, only to find yourself scrolling through websites that promote New Age beliefs. And get this—a lot of what you'll read there will make sense! This is because Satan uses several methodologies to deceive people, which include, but are not limited to:

1. Giving people a whole lot of truth with a hint of lies. Remember, the Bible says a little leaven leavens the

lump. In other words, a little sin will contaminate the entire batch of bread.

2. Giving people a whole lot of lies and seasoning those lies with some truths. He loves to use truths as an outer shell to cover up the lies; this way, he can advance from the conscious to the subconscious.

3. Rewording what the Bible says and repackaging it as his own revelation. For example, the concept of karma comes from Galatians 6:7, which reads, "Be not deceived; God is not mocked: for whatsoever a man soweth, that shall he also reap."

4. Re-branding medical and scientific findings, especially facts established by psychologists. He then rewords and renames these facts and publishes them under a pagan religion so that the religion can appear to be credible.

5. Using celebrities who are determined to remain relevant to promote demonic ideologies and establish cultures centered around those beliefs.

6. Using believers who have not sanctified themselves or, better yet, set themselves apart from the world to promote and normalize demonic cultures amongst believers. He first desensitizes them to sin by taking a tour of their voids, learning what it is that they want, promising to give them whatever it is that they're hungry for, and then provoking them to promote their beliefs publicly. From there, they begin to challenge and threaten any other believer who promotes the truth. This creates a divide in the church's structure,

which often results in the further splitting of believers and the establishment of new religions or, at minimum, new denominations.

Please note that many of the people who are locked away in mental institutions are prophetic people who didn't know who they were, so they turned to many other mediums in their attempts to find themselves. Many of the people who are drug addicts today are empaths; they are prophetic people who don't know how to manage their sensitivity. Because of this, they've experienced so much hurt, rejection and trauma that they turned to drugs to numb the pain. What this means is that the Jezebel spirit is still murdering prophets and prophetic people to this day. Why is this spirit so effective in going after God's mouthpieces? The answer is found in Hosea 4:6, where God says, "My people are destroyed for lack of knowledge; because you have rejected knowledge, I reject you from being a priest to me. And since you have forgotten the law of your God, I also will forget your children." Please note that:

1. The priest represented man before God.
2. The prophet represented God before man.

The short of it is—we can't charge into a church and say, "I just realized that I'm prophetic. What ministry can I serve on?" You need knowledge; you need to study and show yourself approved for the mantle you are assigned to wear. Unfortunately, many prophetic people become fascinated with platforms, mics and fame so-much-so that they rush the process. They go into churches and when they don't get the attention they want fast enough, they claim to have been hurt by the church. They then rush off to another church and then another, until they finally settle in the belief that they are a unique type of prophet; many are deceived into believing that they are modern-day Pauls sent into the Earth to expose the wrongs done in the church. Consequently, they build their ministry by attempting to destroy other ministries. In other words, they begin to come against and tear down the institution that they were designed to defend and to build. They fall into the trap of dishonor, and before long, they start becoming paranoid, thinking that people are after them. Most pastors have seen this happen to people one too many times! And this was a result of them not wanting to die to themselves and their own ambitions, but instead, they decided to make a name for themselves. After a while, they became mystical and spooky. Some could even be found walking down busy streets, holding up huge cardboard signs that read "You're going to hell" and angrily yelling, "Repent" at every passerby who looks like he or she is unsaved. They lost the soundness of their minds because Satan tempted them outside of God's will using a concoction of impatience, rejection, entitlement and vengeance, and when these ingredients came together, they produced ambition. The person then obsessed over thoughts of fame, often imagining themselves being honored in front of the people who hurt and rejected them. These types of imaginations must be cast down. Remember, what you don't cast down will ultimately have to be cast out!

What I'm saying is:

1. Get to know your God. And not religiously, but intimately.
2. Get to know yourself. You are wired a certain way, and as long as you are unaware of this wiring, the enemy will continue to catch you off guard.
3. Get to know your assignment. Your assignment is the method by which you are designed to impact this Earth and destroy Satan's systems.

And please don't rush the process! Get into a good, Godly church home and let God heal and mature you. Don't be in a hurry to know who you are or you'll be in an even bigger hurry to get into ministry. Take your time and study, study, study the Word of God. When the time is right, God will bring you forward (if you do not quit) and He will explain the many mysteries that is your life! And when He does, everything you've ever experienced, felt and desired will all make sense! I'm a living witness to this! And remember, you're more than just an empath. You were specifically created to feel the presence of God and express His heart to His people. This is where your joy is. This is where your peace is. Everything that you've ever wanted is locked up in your assignment. Wake up and get on post. You are needed!

Journal